1st EDITION

Perspectives on Modern World History

The Rwandan Genocide

1st EDITION

Perspectives on Modern World History

The Rwandan Genocide

Alexander Cruden

Editor

GREENHAVEN PRESS
A part of Gale, Cengage Learning

GALE
CENGAGE Learning

Detroit • New York • San Francisco • New Haven, Conn • Waterville, Maine • London

Christine Nasso, *Publisher*
Elizabeth Des Chenes, *Managing Editor*

© 2010 Greenhaven Press, a part of Gale, Cengage Learning.

Gale and Greenhaven Press are registered trademarks used herein under license.

For more information, contact:
Greenhaven Press
27500 Drake Rd.
Farmington Hills, MI 48331-3535
Or you can visit our Internet site at gale.cengage.com.

For product information and technology assistance, contact us at
Gale Customer Support, 1-800-877-4253.

For permission to use material from this text or product, submit all requests online at
www.cengage.com/permissions.

Further permissions questions can be e-mailed to permissionrequest@cengage.com.

Articles in Greenhaven Press anthologies are often edited for length to meet page requirements. In addition, original titles of these works are changed to clearly present the main thesis and to explicitly indicate the author's opinion. Every effort is made to ensure that Greenhaven Press accurately reflects the original intent of the authors. Every effort has been made to trace the owners of copyrighted material.

Cover image © Patrick Robert/Sygma/Corbis and © Charles Caratini/Sygma/Corbis.

LIBRARY OF CONGRESS CATALOGING-IN-PUBLICATION DATA

The Rwandan genocide / Alexander Cruden, book editor.
   p. cm. -- (Perspectives on modern world history)
   Includes bibliographical references and index.
   ISBN 978-0-7377-5007-2 (hardcover)
  1. Genocide--Rwanda--History--20th century--Juvenile literature. 2. Rwanda--History--Civil War, 1994--Juvenile literature. 3. Rwanda--Ethnic relations--History--20th century--Juvenile literature. I. Cruden, Alex.
   DT450.435.R826 2010
   967.57104'31--dc22   2010010290

Printed in the United States of America
2 3 4 5 6 7 14 13 12 11 10

CONTENTS

YA
967.571
R 94
2010

CHAPTER 1   Historical Background on the Rwandan Genocide

In April 1994, a bipartisan congressional group urged President Bill Clinton to lead an active U.S. intervention to save lives in Rwanda. The White House expressed strong concern, but said ending the violence was a Rwandan or United Nations responsibility.

UN peacekeeping mission in Rwanda. The general confronted severe moral choices in life or death situations.

ten—were jailed as genocide suspects. What to do about the accused children, legally as well as morally, presented a dilemma.

CHAPTER 3   Personal Narratives

FOREWORD

"History cannot give us a program for the future, but it can give us a fuller understanding of ourselves, and of our common humanity, so that we can better face the future."
—*Robert Penn Warren,*
American poet and novelist

The history of each nation is punctuated by momentous events that represent turning points for that nation, with an impact felt far beyond its borders. These events—displaying the full range of human capabilities, from violence, greed, and ignorance to heroism, courage, and strength—are nearly always complicated and multifaceted. Any student of history faces the challenge of grasping the many strands that constitute such world-changing events as wars, social movements, and environmental disasters. But understanding these significant historic events can be enhanced by exposure to a variety of perspectives, whether of people involved intimately or of ones observing from a distance of miles or years. Understanding can also be increased by learning about the controversies surrounding such events and exploring hot-button issues from multiple angles. Finally, true understanding of important historic events involves knowledge of the events' human impact—of the ways such events affected people in their everyday lives—all over the world.

Perspectives on Modern World History examines global historic events from the twentieth-century onward by presenting analysis and observation from numerous vantage points. Each volume offers high school, early college level, and general interest readers a thematically arranged anthology of previously published materials that address a major historical event, with an emphasis on international coverage. Each volume opens with background information on the event, then presents the controversies surrounding that event, and concludes with first-person narratives from people who lived through the event or were affected by it. By providing primary sources from the time of the event, as well as relevant commentary surrounding the event, this series can be used to inform debate, help develop critical thinking skills, increase global awareness, and enhance an understanding of international perspectives on history.

Material in each volume is selected from a diverse range of sources, including journals, magazines, newspapers, nonfiction books, personal narratives, speeches, congressional testimony, government documents, pamphlets, organization newsletters, and position papers. Articles taken from these sources are carefully edited and introduced to provide context and background. Each volume of Perspectives on Modern World History includes an array of views on events of global significance. Much of the material comes from international sources and from U.S. sources that provide extensive international coverage.

Each volume in the Perspectives on Modern World History series also includes:

- A full-color **world map**, offering context and geographic perspective.
- An annotated **table of contents** that provides a brief summary of each essay in the volume.
- An **introduction** specific to the volume topic.
- For each viewpoint, a brief **introduction** that has notes about the author and source of the viewpoint, and that provides a summary of its main points.
- Full-color **charts**, **graphs**, **maps**, and other visual representations.

- Informational **sidebars** that explore the lives of key individuals, give background on historical events, or explain scientific or technical concepts.
- A **glossary** that defines key terms, as needed.
- A **chronology** of important dates preceding, during, and immediately following the event.
- A **bibliography** of additional books, periodicals, and Web sites for further research.
- A comprehensive **subject index** that offers access to people, places, and events cited in the text.

Perspectives on Modern World History is designed for a broad spectrum of readers who want to learn more about not only history but also current events, political science, government, international relations, and sociology—students doing research for class assignments or debates, teachers and faculty seeking to supplement course materials, and others wanting to improve their understanding of history. Each volume of Perspectives on Modern World History is designed to illuminate a complicated event, to spark debate, and to show the human perspective behind the world's most significant happenings of recent decades.

INTRODUCTION

How was it that Rwandans—the people of a generally orderly country once known as the Switzerland of Africa—killed a million fellow citizens in just three months? How could they do that to themselves?

The questions are profound for students, historians, social scientists, humanitarians, religious thinkers, political leaders, and advocates of democracy. What enables a seemingly nonviolent person to cross the line and go along with the ultimate violence?

One starting point for understanding may be found in studies conducted with college students in the United States in the 1960s. These studies showed that students could be persuaded to inflict seemingly lethal shocks to other people—people who had done nothing more than answer questions incorrectly. In the most famous of such studies, conducted by Stanley Milgram, the students were instructed to jolt participants for their incorrect answers—first small doses of electricity, then gradually larger. Ultimately, with the encouragement of authority figures and despite the apparent severe suffering, about 65 pecent of the students went on to administer shocks they thought were more than 450 volts, a fatal intensity. In reality, no one was harmed. Unbeknownst to those inflicting the "shocks," the suffering was simulated.

A notable aspect of these studies is that the participants—the students doing the shocking and those being shocked—were of similar social backgrounds, as with the killers and victims in Rwanda. Another profound illustration of what a group of ordinary humans can do to others occurred during World War II. In 1942, a unit of about 500 men was drawn from Hamburg, Germany, and assigned by the Nazis to kill Jewish people in Poland. The 500 were:

> family men too old to be drafted into the army, from working-class and lower middle-class backgrounds, with no military police experience, just raw recruits sent to Poland without warning of, or any training in, their secret mission—the total extermination of all Jews living in the remote villages of Poland. In just four months they had shot to death at point blank range at least 38,000 Jews,

writes Stanford professor Philip G. Zimbardo in his contribution to the 2004 book *The Social Psychology of Good and Evil.*

When the mission began, the German recruits were told any of them could decline to kill the women, children, and men brought before them. Initially, about half chose that option. But as they saw their comrades carry out executions, most of the other half joined in. By the end of the four months, 90 percent participated, according to Nazi records unearthed by British historian Christopher Browning.

The executioners were men without any known murderous tendencies, "until they were put into a situation in which they had official permission and encouragement to act sadistically and brutishly against those arbitrarily labeled as the 'enemy,'" Zimbardo writes. Again, parallels exist in Rwanda.

Zimbardo is among researchers concluding that situational circumstances tend to outweigh whether an individual is in essence good or evil. With all individuals having the capacity for both good and evil, in certain situations many people generally thought of as good go along with and even incite horrific behavior.

Such a situation evolved over decades of the twentieth century in Rwanda. Extremists on both sides emphasized the differences between people of the two main ethnic groups, Hutu and Tutsi. This differentiation was abetted by colonial policies and continued after the nation became independent in 1962. From time to time between that time and the genocide of 1994 there were massacres by both sides, killings ranging from a few dozen people to about two thousand.

"The fluidity with which the Hutu and the Tutsi alternated in the antithetical roles of perpetrator and victim is a hallmark of this genocide. The cyclical character of the atrocities created the requisite dynamics for this phenomenon of role-reversals and interchangeability of roles," writes Vahakn N. Dadrian in the *Journal of Genocide Research*.

This cycle of vengeance gradually acclimated Rwandans to ethnic killing as something acceptable, or at least justifiable, laying the groundwork for what turned into the 100-day genocide. When the spark came—the death of the president in a plane crash—extremists including government leaders used their authority and then peer pressure to persuade tens of thousands of Rwandans to slaughter their neighbors.

Remarkably, the killing was done not just by young men, the population sector that generally carries out armed insurrections, gang warfare, and other organized violence. "The elderly, children, and women were swept up in the slaughter from its very first hours," Adam Jones writes in the *Journal of Genocide Research*. "The extensive role of women in perpetrating the Rwandan genocide is apparently without parallel in recorded history." There was even an aura of "festival," René Lemarchand writes in the journal, with pillaging accompanying the killings and middle-class and professional Rwandans profiting in the massacres.

In sum, the actions of the genocide perpetrators were met with a substantial sense of social acceptance. Encouraged by authority figures, goaded by extremists on radio programs, and facing community pressure to participate or be killed themselves, many ordinary Rwandans—for the most part normally peaceful Christians—allowed the circumstances to turn them into killers. The power of the situation is underscored by the fact that the killing was almost all face-to-face and personal, done by machete, not by remote bombing or in unseen concentration camps.

The viewpoints that follow in this book offer a variety of insights and facts about one of world history's most terrifying events, examining in particular the many factors that contributed to the circumstances of the Rwandan genocide and offering personal narratives of those directly affected.

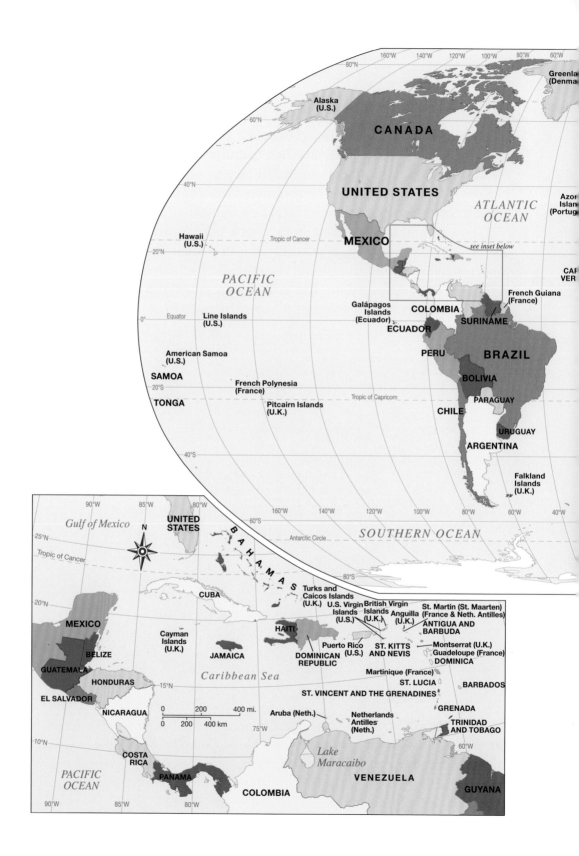

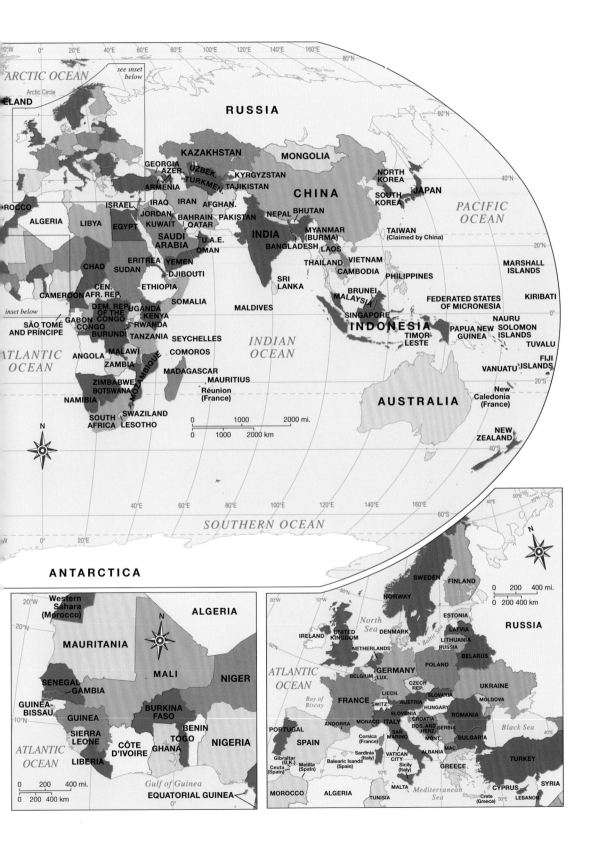

CHAPTER 1

Historical Background on the Rwandan Genocide

An Overview of the Rwandan Genocide

Timothy Longman

In the following selection, Timothy Longman explains that violence between the two main ethnic groups in Rwanda—the Hutus and the Tutsis—was long-standing. Tensions took hold after Belgian colonization in 1917. Relatively small-scale killings also occurred in the decade after the country became independent in 1962. Tensions grew again in the 1980s, and then in the early 1990s turned into warfare and a rapidly executed genocide, followed by counterattacks. Throughout the period, Longman explains, Rwandan leaders from both ethnic groups at times sought compromise and peace, and at other times instigated repression and massacres. Longman, a professor of political science and African studies at Vassar College, has written extensively about conflicts in central Africa. His research includes time spent in Rwanda, Burundi, Congo, Tanzania, Uganda, Kenya, and South Africa.

Photo on previous page: The April 6, 1994, death of Rwanda's president, Juvénal Habyarimana, embroiled the country in genocide. (**Scott Peterson/Getty Images.**)

SOURCE. Timothy Longman, *Encyclopedia of Genocide and Crimes Against Humanity*. Belmont, CA: Macmillan Reference USA, 2005. Copyright © 2005 by Gale Group. Reproduced by permission of Gale, a part of Cengage Learning.

The 1994 genocide in Rwanda represents one of the clearest cases of genocide in modern history. From early April 1994 through mid-July 1994, members of the small Central African state's majority Hutu ethnic group systematically slaughtered members of the Tutsi ethnic minority. An extremist Hutu regime, fearing the loss of its power in the face of a democracy movement and a civil war, made plans for the elimination of all those—moderate Hutu as well as Tutsi—it perceived as threats to its authority. The genocide ended only when a mostly Tutsi rebel army occupied the country and drove the genocidal regime into exile. Over a period of only one hundred days, as many as one million people lost their lives in the genocide and war—making the Rwandan slaughter one of the most intense waves of killing in recorded history.

The origins of ethnic identity in Rwanda remain a subject of considerable controversy. Nearly all scholars agree that populations having the designations Hutu, Tutsi, and Twa existed in the pre-colonial Rwandan state (prior to 1895); however, the exact historic and demographic meanings of these designations remain contested. . . .

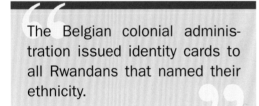

The Belgian colonial administration issued identity cards to all Rwandans that named their ethnicity.

Many current politicians in Rwanda, as well as some scholars, hold the theory that, in pro-colonial Rwanda, Tutsi, Hutu, and Twa were categories that derived from work-related activity and possessed little social significance—citing that the groups shared a common language and culture and lived among one another throughout the territory. According to this theory, colonial policies and ideologies subsequently transformed these categories into ethnic identities.

Proponents of [another] theory believe that the terms Tutsi, Hutu, and Twa conferred status and were freighted with status difference even in pre-colonial Rwanda. Beginning in the mid-1800s, the central court of the kingdom of Rwanda used the categorization of population by ethnicity as a means of extending its control, installing an elite Tutsi class in marginal areas of the kingdom to represent the court. According to this theory, the development of Tutsi dominance that had begun in the late pre-colonial period was accelerated by colonial rule. Colonization transformed group identities via the introduction of Western ideas of race and discrimination on the basis of ethnicity that endowed those identities with greater meaning than they had held previously.

Early Instances of Ethnic Violence

Rwanda was colonized by Germany, which ceded the region to the Belgians during World War I. Supporters of the two theories of the origins of Rwandan ethnic identity agree that violent conflict along ethnic lines rarely, if ever, occurred in pre-colonial Rwanda, and that German and Belgian colonial policies exacerbated the already existing divisions among Hutu, Tutsi, and Twa. Catholic missionaries, who arrived in Rwanda in 1900, influenced the development of ethnic identity in Rwanda. They believed that Rwanda had three distinct racial groups. The Tutsi were supposedly a Hamitic group—tall, thin, of aristocratic demeanor, and more closely related to Europeans (and therefore destined to rule over inferior races). The Hutu were supposedly a Bantu group—shorter and stronger and (purportedly) fit for manual labor. The Twa were considered a Pygmy group—very small and dark and inferior to other peoples.

These interpretations ultimately shaped how Rwandans saw themselves and understood their group identities; moreover, they had become a basis for policies. German and Belgian colonial administrators practiced ethnic group-based indirect rule. They put power in the hands of Tutsi and gave administrative and political positions to Tutsi, and at the same time eliminated the power of Hutu kings and chiefs. The Belgian colonial administration issued identity cards to all Rwandans that named their ethnicity. In addition, the Belgian colonial law of Rwanda dictated that one's ethnicity was the ethnicity of one's father—which effectively eliminated the prior fluid nature of ethnic identities. Occupational and educational opportunities were reserved for Tutsi, whereas Hutu were required to provide forced labor for the Tutsi chiefs. As a result of these and other policies, the Hutu population of Rwanda became increasingly impoverished and embittered. In the 1950s a Hutu elite, supported by progressive Catholic missionaries, emerged to challenge the inequality of Rwandan society. In 1959 a Hutu uprising drove Tutsi chiefs from their positions and thousands of Tutsi citizens of Rwanda into exile. The uprising marked the beginning of the transfer of political power to the majority Hutu. Rwanda gained its independence in 1962. The Hutu-dominated post-independence governments referred to the 1959 uprising as a social revolution. (The current Rwandan government refers to the turbulent events of 1959 as Rwanda's first instance of genocide—though in fact few Tutsi were killed at that time.)

In 1962 Grégoire Kayibanda, the leader of the Party of the Movement for the Emancipation of Hutu (Parmehutu), became Rwanda's president. Kayibanda used ethnic appeals to build his support—thereby creating a tense social environment. When rebel groups that had taken form among the exiled Tutsi attacked the country several times in the early 1960s, Rwandan troops responded by massacring thousands of Tutsi. Thousands more were driven into exile. Ethnic violence erupted in Rwanda again in 1973, partially in response to the 1972 genocide of educated Hutu in neighboring Burundi (which had an ethnic composition similar to that of Rwanda), where Tutsi had retained control. The resulting social disruption in Rwanda was a factor that contributed to the July 1973 coup d'etat that installed army chief Juvénal Habyarimana as the president of Rwanda.

Under Habyarimana, ethnic tensions in Rwanda initially diminished, as the regime focused on attracting international assistance for economic development. The establishment of ethnic quotas in education and employment (which shrank opportunities for Tutsi) appeased Hutu, and the creation of a single political party, the National Revolutionary Movement for Development (MRND), sharply constrained potentially inflammatory political activity. Tutsi were still required to carry identity cards and faced discrimination, but active ethnic tensions diminished. The resulting political calm attracted both internal and international support for Habyarimana, and allowed a decade of steady economic growth.

Friction Grows Between Hutu and Tutsi

By the mid-1980s, however, among Rwandans, frustration with the Habyarimana regime was on the rise. A collapse in the price of coffee, Rwanda's main export, caused a sharp economic downturn and a massive increase in youth unemployment. In the context of economic decline and a growing gap between rich and poor, increasingly apparent corruption among officials in the Habyarimana regime became a growing source of criticism. Preferential treatment for Hutu from Habyarimana's home region of northern Rwanda angered both southern Hutu and Tutsi from throughout the country. In 1990 public frustration manifested itself in a democracy movement that called for expanded civil rights, a legalization of multiparty politics, and free and fair elections. Facing growing unrest, President Habyarimana announced that he would consent to limited political reforms.

The October 1990 invasion of Rwanda by the Rwandan Patriotic Front (RPF) changed the political equation in the country, as it both further compromised the security of the regime and provided an opportunity for Habyarimana and his cohorts to regain popular support by playing the ethnic card. The RPF was a rebel group composed primarily of Tutsi refugees seeking the right to return to Rwanda. Since the beginnings of anti-Tutsi violence in Rwanda in 1959, tens of thousands of Tutsi had been living as refugees, primarily in the neighboring states of Zaire (present-day Democratic Republic of Congo), Burundi, and Uganda—countries in which their safety was precarious. In 1982 persecution of Tutsi by the regime of President Milton Obote in Uganda led thousands of Tutsi to try to return to Rwanda. They were turned away at the border: the Habyarimana regime claimed that there was no room for them in Rwanda. In Uganda, a number of Rwandan Tutsi joined the rebel movement that carried Yoweri Museveni to power in 1986, which afforded them political influence even as they remained vulnerable in that country. It was Tutsi within Museveni's National Resistance Army that had founded the RPF, which received clandestine support from the Museveni regime.

> Habyarimana and his supporters used a cunning two-pronged strategy to improve their political position.

The initial RPF attack on Rwanda's northeastern frontier, on October 1, 1990, was easily quelled by troops of the Habyarimana regime, with the support of troops from Zaire, Belgium, and France. Nevertheless, Habyarimana used the invasion to retake the political lead. On the night of October 4, his supporters in the military staged what appeared to be an attack by the RPF on Kigali [the capital city]. This bogus attack was used to justify the arrest of thousands of prominent Tutsi and moderate Hutu, under the accusation of their being RPF accomplices. At the same time, regime officials organized massacres of Tutsi in several communities in the north of

the country, which they portrayed as spontaneous popular revenge killings in response to the RPF attack. These
assaults served to fan the flames of the ethnic tensions in
the country.

Over the next several years, Habyarimana and his
supporters used a cunning two-pronged strategy to
improve their political position. On the one hand, they
appeased critics by entering into negotiations with the
RPF and offering political concessions, including the
legalization of opposition parties and the creation of a
government of (ostensible) national unity. Yet on the
other hand they actively undermined these concessions.
They denied opposition politicians real political power
as they simultaneously blamed them for any problems
that the country faced, such as the economic decline
and the growing unemployment resulting from the
civil war and an International Monetary Fund (IMF)—
imposed austerity program and currency devaluation.
Habyarimana's supporters encouraged acts of violence
between the members of opposing political parties and
were complacent toward an increase in overall criminal
violence, then blamed the growing insecurity on the
shift to multi-party politics. They appealed to anti-
Tutsi sentiments (which had been intensified by the
RPF invasion), and characterized all members of the
anti-government opposition as RPF sympathizers. Each
time negotiations with the RPF were on the verge of a
breakthrough, Habyarimana's allies instigated small-
scale massacres of Tutsi in various parts of the country
and in general used ethnic violence to further inflame
ethnic tensions. These massacres ultimately served as
dress rehearsals for the eventual genocide, and were part
of a strategy of mobilizing the population and motivat-
ing it further in the direction of violence. Throughout
this period, Habyarimana's supporters increased their
coercive power through a massive expansion of the
Armed Forces of Rwanda (FAR).

MAP OF RWANDA

The boundaries and names shown and the designations used on this map do not imply official endorsement or acceptance by the United Nations.

UGANDA

DEMOCRATIC
REPUBLIC OF THE
CONGO

Butaro
Kidaho
Ruhengeri
Busogo
Kora
Kagali • Mutura
Gisenyi
Nyundo
Kabaya
Ngaru

Kirambe
NORTHERN
PROVINCE
Nemba
Rushashi
Ngororero
Kiyumba

N

WESTERN
PROVINCE

Lac Kivu

Run
Bulinga
Gitarama

Mabanza
Kibuye
Gishyita
Bwakira
Rwamatamu

Birambo

SOUTHERN
PROVINCE

Masango
Gatagara
Ruhang
Nyanza

Kaduha

Rwesero

Karaba
Gikongoro
Karama
Rusatir

Cyangugu
Cyimbogo
Nyakabuye

Rwumba
Kitabi

Butara
Gisagara

Ruramba
Busoro
Munini
Runyombyi

Bugarama

Taken from: United Nations, Department of Field Support, Cartographic Section, June 2008.

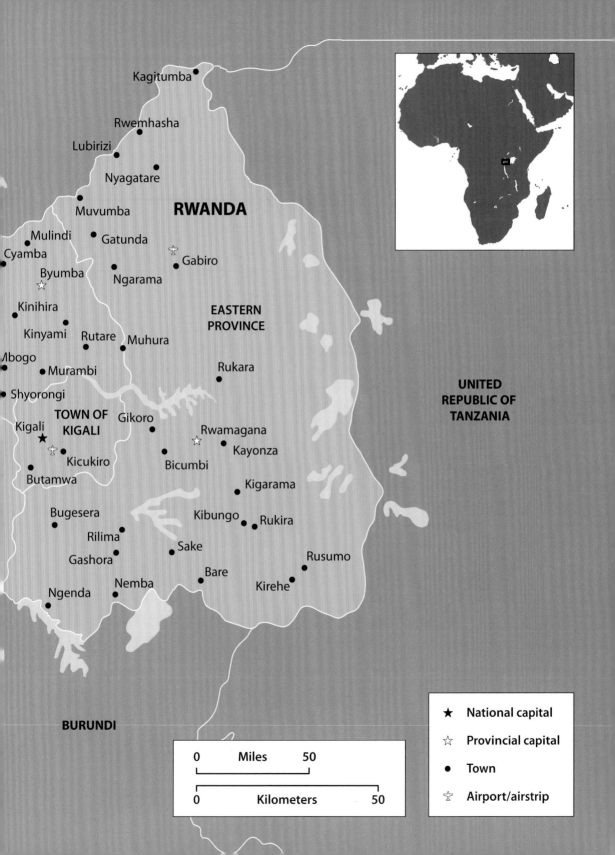

The Road to Genocide

Within the powerful clique close to Habyarimana known as the *akazu*, the idea of retaking broad political control via the setting off of large-scale massacres of any and all persons they regarded as threats to the Habyarimana regime was apparently first proposed sometime in 1992. The *akazu* was composed primarily of individuals from Habyarimana's home region in the north of Rwanda, and included descendants of Hutu chiefs who had been displaced by Tutsi during the colonial period—such as some of the relatives of Habyarimana's wife Agathe Kazinga, who for this reason had retained great personal animosity toward Tutsi. Members of the *akazu* had acquired significant personal wealth and power under Habyarimana's rule, and they were feeling increasingly threatened by political reforms and negotiations with the RPF. Some in the *akazu*—allegedly by mid-1993—had devised a plan to eliminate both Tutsi and moderate Hutu as a final solution to the threats against themselves.

A series of events in 1993 shifted popular support in favor of the Habyarimana regime, supplying the popular base that would make the genocide possible. Massacres of Tutsi in the prefectures of Gisenyi and Kibuye in January triggered a major RPF offensive in February, which captured a large swath of territory in northern Rwanda and displaced a million people (mostly Hutu) from the Ruhengeri and Byumba prefectures. With so many people having been displaced and rumors of civilian massacres in areas controlled by the RPF beginning to swirl, public opinion in Rwanda shifted sharply against the RPF. Even as the Habyarimana regime feigned participation in peace negotiations with the RPF and other opposition parties, it sought to undermine the negotiations by fostering anti-Tutsi and anti-RPF sentiments and attributing any concessions it made to the participation of opposition politicians. This strategy effectively split each of the opposition parties, thereby

The First Reports on the Massacre

The international charity group Oxfam was among the first to confirm genocide was under way in Rwanda. On April 28, 1994, Oxfam declared that systematic killing of as many as half a million Tutsis was taking place.

Oxfam's emergencies officer, Maurice Herson, said Tutsis in southern Rwanda, trying to flee to neighboring Burundi, either "are being hunted and killed or they will starve. They face extermination."

A spokesman for the International Committee of the Red Cross, Tony Burgener, described the situation as "the heart of darkness," according to *The Times* of London, a statement that echoed the title of Joseph Conrad's famous novella set in central Africa.

preventing the installation of a new unity government of transition and realigning many southern Hutu with Habyarimana. The final peace agreement, known as the Arusha Accords, signed in August 1993, was widely perceived within Rwanda as having ceded too much to the RPF and having solidified the division of political parties into pro-Arusha Accords and anti-Arusha Accords wings. The anti-Arusha Accords party factions joined with Habyarimana's MRND and the extreme anti-Tutsi party named the Coalition for the Defense of the Republic (CDR) in a loose pro-regime coalition that called itself "Hutu Power." . . .

Both political and ethnic tensions continued to rise in Rwanda in early 1994. Even as provisions of the Arusha Accords were being implemented, Hutu Power forces sought to scuttle the final transfer of power to a new unity government. The United Nations (UN) Assistance Mission in Rwanda (UNAMIR) stationed international troops in the country to oversee the transition; a battalion of six hundred RPF troops was stationed in Kigali. Rather than reduce its forces, the FAR continued to expand in size and acquire arms—receiving weaponry from France, Egypt, and South Africa. In February Faustin Twagiramungu, the transitional prime minister named in the Arusha Accords, narrowly escaped an assassination attempt, while Féllicien Gatabazi, the executive secretary of the moderate Social Democratic Party, was assassinated. In response, a crowd that had assembled in Gatabazi's home commune lynched the national chairman of the CDR, Martin Bucyana. These political assassinations intensified the sense of crisis in the country and set the stage for the genocide. Intelligence reports coming out of the United States, France, and Belgium in early 1994 all warned that ethnic and political massacres were an imminent possibility in Rwanda. The commander of UNAMIR forces, General Roméo Dallaire, sent a memo to UN headquarters informing them that he had been informed of the existence of the secret plans of Hutu extremists to carry out genocide. None of these warnings were heeded.

The Genocide

On April 6, 1994, the plane carrying President Habyarimana and Cyprien Ntaryamira, the president of Burundi, who were returning from a meeting in Tanzania that had focused on the implementation of the Arusha Accords, was shot down by surface-to-air missiles as it approached the airport in Kigali, and all on board were killed. The downing of the plane remains shrouded in mystery, since the Rwandan military restricted access to the area of the crash and blocked all serious investigation. Although associates of Habyarimana initially blamed the RPF for the assassination, many other observers believed that troops close to the president had carried out the attack—possibly because of an awareness of Habyarimana's reluctance to permit the plans for genocide (of which he was alleged to have been aware) to move forward, or the perception that he had been too moderate in his attitude toward the RPF. In part because of evidence that was eventually presented before the International Criminal Tribunal for Rwanda (ICTR), many political experts now believe that the RPF, frustrated at the president's resistance toward implementing the Arusha Accords, did in fact fire the rockets that brought down Habyarimana's plane.

> " Far from being a spontaneous popular uprising, the 1994 genocide had been carefully planned and coordinated by a small group of government and military officials. "

Whoever was responsible for the crash, the assassination of Habyarimana served as the spark that set the plans for genocide in motion. Within hours of the crash, members of the presidential guard and other elite troops—carrying hit lists composed of the names of persons perceived to be RPF sympathizers, including prominent Tutsi and Hutu opposition politicians and civil society activists—were spreading throughout the capital. On the morning of April 7, the presidential guard assassinated the Prime Minister, Agathe Uwilingiyimana, a moderate Hutu, along with ten Belgian UNAMIR troops who had been guarding her. On the first day of the genocide, death squads also killed leaders of the predominantly Tutsi Liberal Party and the multiethnic Social Democratic Party, several cabinet ministers, justices of the constitutional court, journalists, human rights activists, and progressive priests.

For the first several days, the murderous attacks took place primarily in Kigali and were focused on prominent individuals, both Hutu and Tutsi, perceived to be opponents of the regime. The international community,

The cause of the plane crash that killed Rwandan president Juvénal Habyarimana remains uncertain, but its consequences were catastrophic. (Scott Peterson/Getty Images.)

at this initial stage of the genocide, construed the violence in Rwanda as an ethnic uprising, a spontaneous popular reaction to the death of the president. Without clearly condemning the political and ethnic violence that was taking place, foreign governments moved to evacuate their nationals from Rwanda. Despite calls from UNAMIR Commander Dallaire to have troop strength increased, the member states of the UN Security Council voted to cut the UNAMIR presence from around 2,500 to a token force of 270, largely because countries such as the United States feared becoming entangled in an intractable conflict that would be reminiscent of the then recent disastrous intervention by the United States in Somalia. Belgium quickly withdrew its forces, and was followed by most other participating countries. From the beginning of the violence, the international community thus promulgated a clear message that it was disinterested and would not act to stop the massacres in Rwanda.

Far from being a spontaneous popular uprising, the 1994 genocide had been carefully planned and coordinated by a small group of government and military officials who used the administrative structure and coercive force of the state to invigorate the genocide and extend it across the country. Following Habyarimana's death, a new interim government composed entirely of Hutu Power supporters had seized control. . . .

The genocide in each community followed a pattern. First, the civilian militias raided Tutsi homes and businesses. Fleeing Tutsi were forced to seek refuge in central locations, such as schools, public offices, and churches, where they had been protected during previous waves of violence. Coordinators of the genocide actively exploited the concept of sanctuary and encouraged Tutsi to gather at these places, offering promises of protection when in fact they were calling Tutsi together for their more efficient elimination. In some communities, a limited number of moderate Hutu were killed early in the violence— as a way of sending a message to other Hutu that they needed to cooperate. Once Tutsi had been gathered, soldiers or police joined with the militia in attacking them: first firing on the crowd and throwing grenades, then systematically finishing off survivors with machetes, axes, and knives. In some cases, buildings teeming with victims were set on fire or demolished. In instances in which communities initially resisted the genocide, militias from neighboring areas arrived on the scene and participated in the attacks until local Hutu joined in the killing. Generally armed only with stones, Tutsi were able to pose effective resistance in only a few locations.

By early May the large-scale massacres were complete, and the genocide in each community moved into a second stage of seeking out survivors. The organizers of the genocide clearly sought in this stage to lessen their own responsibility by implicating a larger segment of society in the killing. Although the massacres were carried out by relatively limited groups of militia members and members of the armed forces, all adult men were expected to participate in roadblocks and nightly patrols.

> "The exact number of people killed in the genocide and war remains disputed, and ranges from 500,000 to over a million."

People passing through roadblocks were required to show their identity cards. If a person's card stated that his or her ethnicity was Tutsi, he or she was killed on the spot. If a person had no card, he or she was assumed to be Tutsi. Persons who looked stereotypically Tutsi were almost certainly killed. The military patrols ostensibly searched for perpetrators, but they actually looked for surviving Tutsi who were hiding in communities. Many Hutu risked their own lives to protect Tutsi friends and family. The patrols searched homes where Tutsi were believed to be hiding, and if Tutsi were found, the patrols sometimes killed both Tutsi and the Hutu who were harboring them. Twa, who were a minuscule minority of the Rwandan population, were rarely targets of the genocide and in many communities participated in the killing in an effort to improve their social status.

Post-Genocide Reconstruction and Reconciliation

From the vantage point of the Hutu Power elite, the genocide, although effective at eliminating internal dissent, proved to be a terrible military strategy, as it drained resources and diverted attention from the RPF assault. Better armed and better organized, the RPF swiftly subdued FAR troops. It advanced across eastern Rwanda, then marched west, capturing the former royal capital Nyanza, on May 29; the provisional capital Gitarama, on June 13; and Kigali, on July 4. As it advanced, the RPF liberated Tutsi still being harbored in large numbers in places such as Nyanza and Kabgayi, but they also carried out civilian massacres in many communities they occupied, sometimes after gathering victims for supposed public meetings. Much of the population fled the RPF advance. As the RPF occupied eastern Rwanda, nearly one million refugees fled into Tanzania, while in July, over one million fled into Zaire.

After initially refusing to intervene in Rwanda and to stop the genocide, the UN Security Council, on May 17, authorized the creation of an expanded international force, UNAMIR II—but by the time the force was ready to deploy, the genocide was over. The RPF, angry at international neglect and believing that it could win an outright victory, rejected the idea of a new international intervention. In mid-June, France, which had been a close ally of the regime that turned genocidal, intervened in Rwanda, supposedly to stop the massacres—but it also wished to prevent an absolute RPF victory. French forces established the "Zone Turquoise" in southeastern Rwanda, which they administered for over a month after the RPF had occupied the rest of Rwanda. Nearly two million people gathered in camps for the internally displaced and came under French protection. The French presence also enabled many of the organizers of the genocide, as well as the armed forces, to flee safely into Zaire with their weapons.

On July 17, 1994, the RPF declared victory and named a new interim government. The post-genocide Rwandan government faced the inordinately daunting task of rebuilding a country that had been devastated by violence. The exact number of people killed in the genocide and war remains disputed, and ranges from 500,000 to over a million, with serious disagreement over the portion killed by the RPF and the portion killed by the genocidal regime. Whatever the exact number of dead, the loss of life was massive and the impact on society immeasurable. The RPF, seeking wider popular support, based the new government loosely on the Arusha

Accords and appointed a multiethnic slate of ministers from the former opposition parties that included a Hutu president and prime minister. Real power, however, remained firmly in RPF hands, with Defense Minister and Vice President Paul Kagame widely acknowledged as the ultimate authority in the country.

The RPF, which became Rwanda's new national army, took as its first main task the taking of control over the territory, which it did with considerable brutality. The RPF summarily executed hundreds of people who were suspected of involvement in the genocide, and arrested thousands more. Following the late August departure of French forces, the RPF sought to close the camps for the internally displaced. It used force in some cases, such as in its attack on the Kibeho camp in April 1995, in which several thousand civilians died. The refugee camps just across the border in Zaire continued to pose a security threat for the new government, as members of the former FAR and citizen militias living in the camps used the camps as a base from which to launch raids on Rwanda. In mid-1996 the RPF sponsored an antigovernment rebellion in eastern Zaire by the Alliance of Democratic Forces for the Liberation of Congo-Zaire (ADFL). The RPF itself attacked the refugee camps. The RPF killed thousands of refugees who sought to go deeper into Zaire rather than return to Rwanda. With support from the RPF and troops from Uganda and Burundi, the ADFL swiftly advanced across Zaire, driving President Mobutu Sese-Sekou from power in early 1997.

The Government Tries for Justice

After taking power, the new government of Rwanda set about rebuilding the country's physical infrastructure, but it also committed itself to reconstructing the society. The establishment of the principle of accountability for the genocide and a repudiation of the principle of impunity were primary goals. By the late 1990s the government had imprisoned 120,000 people under the accusation of participation in the genocide. Although considerable effort was put into rebuilding the judicial system, trials of persons accused of genocide proceeded very slowly—beginning only in December 1996 and with fewer than five thousand cases tried by 2000. Responding to the need to expedite trials, but also hoping more effectively to promote accountability and reconciliation, the government decided in 2000 to implement a new judicial process, called *gacaca*, based loosely on a traditional Rwandan dispute resolution mechanism. The new *gacaca* courts, the first of which began to operate in June 2002, consist of panels of popularly elected lay judges from every community in the country. The panels preside at public meetings, at which all but the most serious genocidal crimes are tried. Beginning in 2003, the government began to release provisionally thousands of people who had had no formal charges brought against them or who had confessed to participation in the genocide (and would therefore be given reduced sentences). In addition to judicial strategies, the government has sought to promote reconciliation by promulgating a revised understanding of Rwandan history that emphasizes a unified national identity; creating reeducation camps for returning refugees, released prisoners, entering university students, and newly elected government officials; establishing memorials and annual commemorations of the genocide; changing the national anthem, flag, and seal; decentralizing the political structure; and adopting a new constitution.

Efforts to promote reconciliation have been undermined by the RPF's continuing mistrust of the population and its desire to retain control. The government has been highly intolerant of dissent, accusing critics of supporting the ideology of division and genocide. The government has harassed, outlawed, and co-opted human rights organizations, religious groups, and other segments of civil society. Journalists have been harassed and arrested. All political parties but the RPF have been tightly controlled. Power has become increasingly concentrated in the hands of the RPF and of [the] Tutsi, and Paul Kagame has amassed and continues to amass increasing personal power. Kagame assumed the presidency in 2000. A putative "democratic transition" in 2003 actually served to consolidate RPF control over Rwanda.

The international community, plagued by guilt over its failure to stop the genocide, has been highly forgiving of the human rights abuses of the RPF, generally treating the abuses as an understandable or even necessary occurrence in the aftermath of genocide. It has given backing and assistance to both the camps in Zaire and the reconstruction of Rwanda. The main outcome of the international reaction to the Rwandan genocide was the creation of the ICTR, based in Arusha, Tanzania. Created by the UN Security Council in late 1994, the ICTR is entrusted with trying the chief organizers of the 1994 genocide as well as RPF officials responsible for war crimes.

Before the Genocide Began, the Perpetrators Had French Support

Alex Duval Smith

In the following selection, Alex Duval Smith asserts that, in the early 1990s, the president of France backed the Hutu leaders of Rwanda, who were even then hunting down the Tutsi part of their population. This circumstance was revealed in long-secret French documents obtained by lawyers representing Tutsi survivors. Smith explains that France's president, François Mitterrand, knew that massacres were under way but wanted to maintain influence in the African nation—despite opposition from some French military and government leaders. An international journalist, Smith often covers stories about Africa.

SOURCE. Alex Duval Smith, "Mitterrand's Role Revealed in Rwandan Genocide Warning," *The Independent* (London), July 3, 2007. Copyright © 2007 Independent Newspapers (UK) Ltd. Reproduced by permission. www.independent.co.uk.

The former French president François Mitterrand supported the perpetrators of the 1994 Rwandan genocide despite clear warnings that mass killings of the Tutsi population were being orchestrated, according to declassified French documents.

The publication of the documents in today's [July 3, 2007] *Le Monde* for the first time confirms long-held suspicions against France. The previously secret diplomatic telegrams and government memos also suggest the late French president was obsessed with the danger of "Anglo-Saxon" influence gripping Rwanda. In three months from April 1994, at least a million Rwandans—mainly Tutsis—were systematically slaughtered in killings engineered by the Hutu regime to exterminate its ethnic rivals and repel the Uganda-trained Rwandan Patriotic Front (RPF).

The documents, obtained by lawyers for six Tutsi survivors who are bringing a case against France for "complicity with genocide" at the Paris Army Tribunal, suggest the late President Mitterrand's support for the Hutus was informed by an obsession with maintaining a French foothold in the region. One of the lawyers, Antoine Compte, said France was aware of the potential danger of its support for the pre-genocide Rwandan government. "Massacres on an ethnic basis were going on and we have evidence that France knew this from at least January 1993. The French military executed the orders of French politicians. The motivation was an obsession with the idea of an Anglo-Saxon plot to oust France from the region."

> France took a strong interest in the country after independence, seeing it as a bulwark against the powerful influences of English-speaking Uganda and Kenya.

Mr Compte said the file of diplomatic messages and initialled presidential memos, obtained from the François Mitterrand Foundation, provided evidence that

Once-secret papers showed that France's president François Mitterrand (foreground) supported the genocidal regime in Rwanda in order to bolster French interests in Africa. (**Pascal Guyot/AFP/Getty Images.**)

the French military in Rwanda were under direct instruction from the Elysée Palace [the official residence of the French president]. The lawyer yesterday called on the investigating judge at the Paris Army Tribunal to interview senior French political figures, including military figures, diplomats, the former defence minister, Pierre Joxe and former prime minister, Alain Juppé.

"It emerges quite clearly from the documents that diplomats, the French secret services, military figures and Mr Joxe wanted France to disengage from Rwanda, or at least to act differently. But the president was obsessed," said Mr Compte.

Reports Indicate France Was Warned

Among the evidence to suggest France was informed of the mounting genocide is a diplomatic telegram from October 1990 in which the French defence attaché in the Rwandan capital Kigali alerts Paris of the "growing number of arbitrary arrests of Tutsis or people close to them." The cable adds: "It is to be feared that [it could] degenerate into an ethnic war."

Another diplomatic memo, sent by French ambassador Georges Martres on 19 January 1993, quotes a Rwandan informant as saying that the president of the country, Juvénal Habyarimana, had suggested "proceeding with a systematic genocide using, if necessary, the army."

Habyarimana was killed on 6 April 1994—the date that marks the start of the genocide—when his plane was shot down over Kigali.

Even though Rwanda was Belgian for most of the colonial era, France took a strong interest in the country after independence, seeing it as a bulwark against the powerful influences of English-speaking Uganda and Kenya.

In the 1980s, French involvement in Rwanda was limited to two dozen military advisers. But when the Uganda-based RPF began launching attacks against President Habyarimana's regime in 1990, France sent arms and troops. Critics claim French troops stood by and watched as Rwandan Hutu soldiers massacred Tutsi civilians.

France claims its military involvement was aimed at aiding Hutu-Tutsi power-sharing. Last year, a French investigating magistrate, Jean-Louis Bruguière, alleged the RPF shot down Habyarimana's aircraft and issued arrest warrants against nine high-ranking officials in the current Rwandan government.

The U.S. Government Debated a Response

Congress of the United States Subcommittee on Africa of the Committee on Foreign Affairs, White House Office of the Press Secretary, Bill Clinton

In the spring of 1994, as reports of widespread killing in Rwanda reached the U.S. government, the House of Representatives Subcommittee on Africa held hearings and then, on April 20, asked the president for American action to stop the bloodshed. This was at a time when the death toll was reported at 20,000, a huge number, but only a tiny fraction of those eventually killed. The White House responded two days later with a public statement that Rwandans themselves should end the killing. A month later, on May 25, President Bill Clinton sent a letter to the subcommittee leader, Representative Eliot Engel, expressing his concern and his support for regional leaders and the United Nations in their efforts to achieve a cessation of violence.

SOURCE. "The Crisis in Rwanda, Hearing Before the Subcommittee on Africa," in Committee on Foreign Affairs, House of Representatives, U.S. Government Printing Office, May 4, 1994, pp. 68–71.

The Subcommittee on Africa Takes a Stand

Dear Mr. President:

We are writing to express our strong support for an active United States role in helping to resolve the crisis in Rwanda. Given the fact that approximately 20,000 people have died thus far [by April 20, 1994] in the tragic conflict, it is important that the United States endeavor to end the bloodshed and to bring the parties to the negotiating table.

We praise American officials at the U.S. embassy in Kigali [Rwanda's capital] and at the Africa Bureau in Washington for their superb performance in the evacuation of American citizens safely from Rwanda. Nevertheless, America must not now disengage from the conflict. The United States is seen by the parties to the dispute as an honest broker. We, therefore, have a critical role to play as an intermediary if the Rwandan conflict is to be resolved.

> Mr. President, the lives of thousands of innocent civilians are at stake.

Only last August, the interim Rwandan government and the Rwandan Patriotic Front (RPF) signed the so-called Arusha Peace Accord, ending three years of war. Since this agreement was reached, however, continuing disputes between the parties have prevented the implementation of the agreement. The killings of the Presidents of Rwanda and Burundi was simply a match which sparked the simmering feud into the present conflagration.

The United Nations and its peacekeeping force in Rwanda, deployed to assist in the execution of the Arusha accord, have done their best to promote a settlement. We are encouraged by the recent United Nations Security Council's decision to keep United Nations peacekeepers

President Bill Clinton was urged by members of Congress to wield American force to quell the Rwandan civil war. (Cynthia Johnson/Time & Life Pictures/Getty Images.)

in Rwanda. Continued U.N. engagement in Rwanda is crucial to peaceful settlement of the Rwandan conflict.

The United States, in cooperation with the United Nations, can play an important role in conflict resolution in Rwanda. In addition, our country can take important measures unilaterally to assist in the peaceful resolution of the conflict in Rwanda, in particular, and the region, in general. First, the United States must make clear to those involved in the killing of innocent civilians that they will be held accountable.

Second, we urge you to inform the parties to the conflict that the U.S. will not recognize any government which assumes control by forceful means.

Mr. President, the lives of thousands of innocent civilians are at stake, and it is important to demonstrate that these individuals are just as worthy of our attention as people affected by conflicts in other parts of the world. We thank you for your prompt statement on the crisis and encourage you to make resolution of this conflict a priority until it is settled peacefully.

Sincerely,
Eliot L. Engel, Dan Burton, Lincoln Diaz-Balart,
Edward R. Royce, Harry Johnston, Donald Payne,
Alcee L. Hastings, Don Edwards, Robert G. Torricelli

Statement by the President's Press Secretary

The President's National Security Advisor, Anthony Lake, met today with Rwandan human rights monitor Monique Mujawamariya at the White House. Mr. Lake expressed his deep satisfaction that Ms. Mujawamarija had escaped harm and expressed deep concern over the violence that continues to rage in Rwanda following the tragic deaths of Rwandan President Habyarimana and Burundian President Ntaryamira two weeks ago. He said that the horrors of civil war and mass killings of civilians since then have shocked and appalled the world community. All responsible officials and military officers must bring offending troops and units under control immediately.

We call on the Rwandan army and the Rwandan Patriotic Front to agree on an immediate ceasefire and return to negotiations called for and facilitated by the Government of Tanzania. We applaud the efforts of regional leaders who are actively engaged in the search for peace and call on the people of the region to support their quest. The United States is prepared to participate, as in the past, in renewed negotiation in the context of the Arusha Agreement of August 4, 1993. The principles of a negotiated agreement and power-sharing in that agreement remain valid bases for a return to peace in Rwanda.

> I share your commitment to bringing an end to the senseless violence that has plagued Rwanda.

We call on the leadership of the Rwandan armed forces, including Army Commander-in-Chief Col. Augustin Bizimungu, Col. Nkundiye, Capt. Pascal Simbikangwa and Col. Bagosora, to do everything in their power to end the violence immediately.

In line with the U.N. Security Council resolution yesterday [April 21, 1994], we believe that the U.N. Assistance Mission for Rwanda (UNAMIR) has an important continued role to perform in Rwanda in attempting to secure a ceasefire between the parties, assisting humanitarian relief operations and protecting Rwandans under their care. We share the belief that the reduction of UNAMIR personnel, in recognition of the need to ensure their safety and security, must not put at risk the lives of Rwandans under U.N. protection.

The President Responds to the House Panel Leader

Dear Eliot:

Thank you for your recent letter expressing support for an active United States role in helping to resolve the crisis in Rwanda.

I share your commitment to bringing an end to the senseless violence that has plagued Rwanda in the weeks since the tragic deaths of the Rwandan and Burundian Presidents. Since that time, our government has been working in support of the efforts of regional leaders and the United Nations to arrange a cease-fire and renew negotiations in the context of the Arusha Agreement of August 1993.

Specifically, we took the initiative to request that President [Ali Hassan] Mwinyi of Tanzania resume the Arusha peace process, urged President Museveni of Uganda to call on the RPF to cease-fire and carried this plea directly to the RPF in Kampala and Washington. We sent an experienced observer to Arusha for the talks which were to have begun April 23, and we will be represented when and if they get underway this week. We have also been in regular contact with the Governments of France and Belgium who share our concern about Rwanda. We also plan to enhance our assistance to humanitarian relief efforts to Rwanda and Burundi.

On April 22, following a meeting between my National Security Advisor, Anthony Lake, and Rwandan human rights monitor Monique Mujawamariya, the White House issued a strong public statement calling for the Rwandan army and the Rwandan Patriotic Front to do everything in their power to end the violence immediately. This followed an earlier statement by me calling for a cease-fire and the cessation of the killings.

As that statement notes, I share your belief that the U.N. Assistance Mission for Rwanda (UNAMIR) still has an important role to play in brokering a cease-fire, assisting humanitarian relief operations and ensuring the safety of Rwandans under their protection.

I also appreciate your kind comments on the superb performance of the personnel at our embassy in Kigali and their counterparts here in Washington to organize and carry out the evacuation of U.S. citizens from

Rwanda. Their tireless efforts ensured the safety of more than 250 Americans.

Thank you again for sharing your thoughts and for your support of this important effort. It is my hope that peace can be restored to Rwanda soon and that Rwanda can return to the path toward national reconciliation and democracy.

Sincerely,
Bill Clinton

American Support Came for UN Prosecutions

Madeleine K. Albright

In the following statement issued on November 8, 1994, after the Rwandan genocide had ended, the U.S. ambassador to the United Nations, Madeleine Albright, urges Rwanda to cooperate with a new UN tribunal for prosecuting genocide participants. She acknowledges that the Security Council did not accommodate all of the Rwandan government's concerns, but asserts the importance of moving forward with the tribunal. Albright recognizes the many challenges facing the tribunal and the Rwandan people, but she expresses the hope that the tribunal can help Rwanda achieve justice and reconciliation. An accompanying UN Security Council resolution calls on all nations to support the tribunal. After her service in the United Nations, Madeleine Albright was the U.S. secretary of state from 1997 to 2001, making her the first woman ever to hold that post.

SOURCE. Madeleine K. Albright, "UN Security Council Establishes International Tribunal for Rwanda," *U.S. Department of State Dispatch*, vol. 5, November 21, 1994, pp. 780–81.

Genocide occurred in Rwanda last spring [1994]. Other grave violations of international humanitarian law also have ravaged that state. This [United Nations Security] Council has been seized with these horrific events through much of this year. The Council itself has not been immune from criticism. But today [November 8, 1994] marks the culmination of months of very hard and persistent work by our respective governments, the Secretariat, the Commission of Experts, and this Council to create a new ad hoc tribunal for the investigation and prosecution of genocide, crimes against humanity, and war crimes in Rwanda and by Rwandan citizens in states neighboring Rwanda.

> The establishment of the International Tribunal for Rwanda is only the beginning.

We regret that the Government of Rwanda cast its vote against the resolution. As other members of the Council have stated, the co-sponsors worked hard to accommodate a number of Rwandan concerns, but we were not able to accommodate all of them. While we understand their concerns regarding several key issues—indeed, on the death penalty we might even agree—it was simply not possible to meet those concerns and still maintain broad support in the Council. Therefore, my government believes that the right choice is to establish the tribunal this tragedy demands rather than wait to achieve an agreement that would never come.

Nonetheless, we urge the Government of Rwanda to honor its obligation to cooperate fully with the International Tribunal and the investigation it must undertake in order to prosecute those guilty of the unspeakable acts of genocide and other atrocities. We appreciate the efforts of the UN Legal Counsel, Hans Corell, to consult with the Government of Rwanda in Kigali [Rwanda's capital city] about this resolution and the statute for the tribunal. Over the last few months, this Council has acted with determination to establish the tribunal at the earliest possible date.

The prosecutor will need to work very closely with the Government of Rwanda to establish a presence in that country and to operate freely in his investigations and prosecutions. My government fully supports the establishment of a tribunal office in Kigali and for a great deal of the tribunal's work necessarily to proceed in Rwanda. We also look forward to further consultations on the official seat of the tribunal. It is imperative that the tribunal operate efficiently, securely, and in a manner consistent with the overall development of international humanitarian law. We will look forward to the views of the Secretary General and the prosecutor in our evaluation.

As Chief Prosecutor, Justice [Richard] Goldstone will bring to this endeavor the same integrity and skill that he already has infused into the International Tribunal for the Former Yugoslavia. We look forward to assisting Justice Goldstone in whatever way we can to facilitate his work on Rwanda. We also look forward to the selection of a Deputy Prosecutor for Rwanda who will have major responsibility for investigations and prosecutions.

The establishment of the International Tribunal for Rwanda is only the beginning. One major challenge ahead of us is adequate funding for the tribunal. We urge all member states to make voluntary contributions. More importantly, the United Nations must provide sufficient funds for these early, critical months of the tribunal's work. We stress, however, that with the growing budgetary needs of the International Tribunal for the Former Yugoslavia, our challenge will be to finance both ad hoc tribunals with enough resources to get the job done.

The judicial system in Rwanda also will require much rebuilding in order to take on the enormous task of daily law enforcement, as well as the prosecution of many of the suspects whom the tribunal will not be able to handle. My government is prepared to assist Rwanda in this important task, and we encourage other governments to provide assistance.

The investigation of genocide is, indeed, very grim work. But we have a responsibility to see that the International Tribunal for Rwanda can accomplish its objective—one that this Council increasingly recognizes to hold individuals accountable for their violations of international humanitarian law. As evident in the former Yugoslavia, in Rwanda there is an equal need to forge harmony among ethnic groups by bringing to justice the individuals who committed such heinous crimes, regardless of their position in society.

U.S. ambassador to the UN Madeleine Albright (far left) lent support in Security Council deliberations to an international tribunal investigating genocide. (Pamela Price/AFP/Getty Images.)

In closing, let me express my government's hope that the step we have taken here today can promote both justice and national reconciliation, lest the Rwandan people be unable to escape the memory of madness and barbarism they have just lived through.

The UN Security Council Resolution

Resolution 955 (November 8, 1994)
The Security Council,

Reaffirming all its previous resolutions on the situation in Rwanda,

Having considered the reports of the Secretary-General pursuant to paragraph 3 of resolution 935 (1994) of 1 July 1994 and having taken note of the reports of the

Special Rapporteur for Rwanda of the United Nations Commission on Human Rights,

Expressing appreciation for the work of the Commission of Experts established pursuant to resolution 935 (1994), in particular its preliminary report on violations of international humanitarian law in Rwanda transmitted by the Secretary-General's letter of 1 October 1994,

Expressing once again its grave concern at the reports indicating that genocide and other systematic, widespread and flagrant violations of international humanitarian law have been committed in Rwanda,

Determining that this situation continues to constitute a threat to international peace and security,

Determined to put an end to such crimes and to take effective measures to bring to justice the persons who are responsible for them,

Convinced that in the particular circumstances of Rwanda, the prosecution of persons responsible for serious violations of international humanitarian law would enable this aim to be achieved and would contribute to the process of national reconciliation and to the restoration and maintenance of peace,

Believing that the establishment of an international tribunal for the prosecution of persons responsible for genocide and the other above-mentioned violations of international humanitarian law will contribute to ensuring that such violations are halted and effectively redressed,

Stressing also the need for international cooperation to strengthen the courts and judicial system of Rwanda, having regard in particular to the necessity for those courts to deal with large numbers of suspects,

Considering that the Commission of Experts established pursuant to resolution 935 (1994) should continue on an urgent basis the collection of information relating to evidence of grave violations of international humanitarian law committed in the territory of Rwanda and should submit its final report to the Secretary-General by 30 November 1994,

Acting under Chapter VII of the Charter of the United Nations,

1. Decides hereby, having received the request of the Government of Rwanda, to establish an international tribunal for the sole purpose of prosecuting persons responsible for genocide and other serious violations of international humanitarian law committed in the territory of Rwanda and Rwandan citizens responsible for genocide and other such violations committed in the territory of neighbouring States, between 1 January 1994 and 31 December 1994 and to this end to adopt the Statute of the International Criminal Tribunal for Rwanda annexed hereto;

2. Decides that all States shall cooperate fully with the International Tribunal and its organs in accordance with the present resolution and the Statute of the International Tribunal and that consequently all States shall take any measures necessary under their domestic law to implement the provisions of the present resolution and the Statute, including the obligation of States to comply with requests for assistance or orders issued by a Trial Chamber under Article 28 of the Statute, and requests States to keep the Secretary-General informed of such measures;

47

3. Considers that the Government of Rwanda should be notified prior to the taking of decisions under Articles 26 and 27 of the Statute;

4. Urges States and intergovernmental and non-governmental organizations to contribute funds, equipment and services to the International Tribunal, including the offer of expert personnel;

5. Requests the Secretary-General to implement this resolution urgently and in particular to make practical arrangements for the effective functioning of the International Tribunal, including recommendations to the Council as to possible locations for the seat of the International Tribunal at the earliest time and to report periodically to the Council;

6. Decides that the seat of the International Tribunal shall be determined by the Council having regard to considerations of justice and fairness as well as administrative efficiency, including access to witnesses, and economy, and subject to the conclusion of appropriate arrangements between the United Nations and the State of the seat, acceptable to the Council, having regard to the fact that the International Tribunal may meet away from its seat when it considers it necessary for the efficient exercise of its functions; and decides that an office will be established and proceedings will be conducted in Rwanda, where feasible and appropriate, subject to the conclusion of similar appropriate arrangements;

7. Decides to consider increasing the number of judges and Trial Chambers of the International Tribunal if it becomes necessary;

8. Decides to remain actively seized of the matter.

VOTE: 13-1-1 (Rwanda against; China abstaining).

An African Investigation Found That World Powers Failed

The International Panel of Eminent Personalities to Investigate the 1994 Genocide in Rwanda and the Surrounding Events

According to the International Panel of Eminent Personalities, a group appointed by the Organization of African Unity, world powers repeatedly failed to prevent, halt, or even diminish the 1994 massacres in Rwanda committed by the Hutu majority against the Tutsi minority. This failure happened even though it would have been relatively easy to save many thousands of lives using just a small military intervention, the panel asserts. Deliberately or not, the United Nations and leading countries, particularly the United States, misunderstood or ignored the realities of the genocide.

The panel was led by Ketumile Masire, president of Botswana, from 1980 to 1998. Members included Amadou Tourmani Toure, Mali's head of state in 1991 and 1992;

Liberian former cabinet member Ellen Johnson Sirleaf (who later became that country's president); UNICEF leaders Lisbet Palme of Sweden and Stephen Lewis of Canada; and P.N. Bhagwati, former chief justice of the Supreme Court of India.

The International Panel of Eminent Personalities to Investigate the 1994 Genocide in Rwanda and the Surrounding Events was created by the Organization of African Unity [OAU]. As the genocide was unprecedented in African annals, so is the Panel. This is the first time in the history of the OAU that Africa's Heads of State and Governments have established a commission that will be completely independent of its creators in its findings and its recommendations. We are honoured by the responsibility that has been entrusted to us.

Throughout our work, which began with a meeting in Addis Ababa in October 1998, we have attempted to function in a manner worthy of this honour and consistent with the gravity of the subject matter. . . .

What the World Could Have Done

If there is anything worse than the genocide itself, it is the knowledge that it did not have to happen. The simple, harsh truth is that the genocide was not inevitable; and that it would have been relatively easy to stop it from happening prior to April 6, 1994, and then to mitigate the destruction significantly once it began. In the words of one expert, [Howard Adelman], "This was the most easily preventable genocide imaginable."

The conspirators may have seemed formidable in local terms, but in fact they were small in number, modestly armed, and substantially dependent on the outside world. On the few occasions when the world did protest against the human rights violations being perpetrated, the abuses largely halted, if temporarily. This has been documented thoroughly. Conversely, each time the world appeased the latest outrage, it enhanced the sense of Hutu Power impunity. Since no one was ever punished for massacres or human rights abuses, since the [President Juvénal] Habyarimana government remained a favourite recipient of foreign aid, and since no one demanded an end to the escalating incitement against the Tutsi, why would Hutu radicals not believe they could get away with just about anything?

> When the Nigerian ambassador complained that too much attention was being paid to cease-fire negotiations and too little to stopping the massacres, he was largely ignored.

The plot leaders were in it for the spoils. Even a hint, let alone a threat, that further aid or loans or arms would not be forthcoming was taken very seriously indeed. Such threats were invoked with success to force Habyarimana to sign the Arusha accords [a 1993 power-sharing peace pact]. They were rarely made in connection with human rights abuses or ethnic persecution, however, and when they were, the threats were never followed up, reflecting the reality that human rights were not high on the agendas of many foreign governments.

Beyond this, some outsiders were blinded by their faith in multipartyism as a panacea for all [of] Rwanda's woes. The atrocities aimed at the Tutsi were mistaken for more violence flowing from the civil war. End the civil war and implement the Arusha accords, they reasoned, and ethnic violence will automatically stop. To forward the goal of peace, it was necessary to remain engaged. Withdrawal of aid was therefore seen as counter-productive.

Few bothered to learn the lesson from Arusha's utter failure that no agreement mattered unless Hutu Power was shattered. Precisely the same crucial analytical error was repeated throughout the period from April to July [1994], when the Security Council and the United

Nations Secretariat consistently took the position that ending the civil war took primacy over ending the genocide. When the Nigerian ambassador complained that too much attention was being paid to cease-fire negotiations and too little to stopping the massacres, he was largely ignored. The Carlsson Inquiry, appointed by UN Secretary-General Kofi Annan in 1999 to look into the role of the UN in the genocide, criticizes the entire UN family for this "costly error of judgment." In fact, this seems to us too generous an interpretation of the world's failure.

A Truce Was the Wrong Goal

Here was a clear-cut case of rote diplomacy by the international community. As the UN's own Department of Peacekeeping Operations later concluded, "A fundamental misunderstanding of the nature of the conflict . . . contributed to false political assumptions and military assessments." Security Council members blithely ignored both the discrete realities of the situation and the urgent advocacy of the nongovernmental agencies who were crying out the truth to whomever would listen. Instead, the automatic reflex was to call for a cease-fire and negotiations, outcomes that would have coincided perfectly with the aims and strategy of the genocidaires. The annihilation of the Tutsi would have continued, while the war between the armies paused, and negotiators wrangled. In reality, anything that slowed the march of the RPF [Rwandan Patriotic Front, a Tutsi-led force] to military victory was a gift to Hutu Power. In the end, its victory alone ended the genocide and saved those Tutsi who were still alive by July. We count Rwanda fortunate that a military truce—the single consistent initiative

> The world did less than nothing. . . . The world powers assembled as the UN Security Council actually chose to reduce, rather than enhance, their presence.

pursued by the international community—was never reached.

It should only have taken the information at hand to formulate a correct response. It may well be that the mass media did not at first grasp the full extent of the genocide, but that was not true of the world's decision-makers. Eyewitness accounts were never lacking, whether from Rwandans or expatriates with the International Committee for the Red Cross, Human Rights Watch, the US Committee for Refugees, or others. Week after week for three months, reports sent directly from Rwanda to home governments and international agencies documented the magnitude of the slaughter and made it plain that this was no tribal bloodletting, but the work of hardline political and military leaders. At the same time, the reports spelled how countless people could still be saved, identifying exactly where they were hiding, and what steps were needed to rescue them. Yet the world did less than nothing. As subsequent chapters fully document, the world powers assembled as the UN

The killings of ten Belgian troops in Rwanda spurred the international community to withdraw its peacekeepers from the warring nation. (Scott Peterson/ Getty Images.)

Security Council actually chose to reduce, rather than enhance, their presence.

The obvious, necessary response was a serious international military force to deter the killers; this seems to us a self-evident truth. This Panel wants to go on record as one that shares the conviction of UN Assistance Mission to Rwanda (UNAMIR) Commander General Romeo Dallaire: "The killings could have been prevented if there had been the international will to accept the costs of doing so. . . . " As we have seen, that will was at best half-hearted before April 6, and it collapsed entirely in the early stages of the genocide. Virtually every authority we know believes that a larger, better-equipped, and toughly mandated force could have played a critical role, possibly in deterring the conspiracy entirely or, at the least, in causing the plotters to modify or stall their plans and in significantly reducing the number of deaths. It seems certain that appropriate UN intervention at any time after the genocide began would have had a major role in stopping the killings.

Dallaire has always insisted that with 5,000 troops and the right mandate, UNAMIR could have prevented most of the killings. In 1998, several American institutions decided to test Dallaire's argument. The Carnegie Commission on Preventing Deadly Conflict, the Institute for the Study of Diplomacy at Georgetown University in Washington, D.C., and the US Army undertook a joint project to consider what impact an international military force was likely to have had. Thirteen senior military leaders addressed the issue, and a report based on their presentations, as well as on other research, was prepared for the Carnegie Commission by Colonel Scott Feil of the US Army. His conclusion was straightforward: "A modern force of 5,000 troops . . . sent to Rwanda sometime between April 7 and April 21, 1994, could have significantly altered the outcome of the conflict . . . forces appropriately trained, equipped and commanded, and introduced in a timely manner, could have stemmed the violence in and around the capital, prevented its spread to the countryside, and created conditions conducive to the cessation of the civil war between the RPF and RGF [Rwandan Government Forces]."

The Response Was Almost Beyond Belief

Of course, we understand that this was a strictly theoretical exercise, and it is easy to be wise after the fact. On the other hand, we have no reason to question the objectivity of this analysis or of any of the participants. Neither they nor the author seem to have had a vested interest in this conclusion. Moreover, even those analyses that have recently stressed the logistic complications in swiftly mobilizing a properly equipped force do not deny that scores of thousands of Tutsi, "up to 125,000," might have been saved at any time during the months of the genocide. By any standard, these American reports stand as a humiliating rebuke to the US government whose influence was so great in ensuring that no adequate force ever was sent.

Rather than respond with appropriate force, the opposite happened, spurred by the murders of the Belgian Blue Berets and Belgium's withdrawal of its remaining troops. Exactly two weeks after the genocide began—following strenuous lobbying for total withdrawal led by Belgium and Britain, and with American UN Ambassador Madeleine Albright advocating the most token of forces and the United States adamantly refusing to accept publicly that a full-fledged, Convention-defined genocide was in fact taking place—the Security Council made the astonishing decision to reduce the already inadequate UNAMIR force to a derisory 270 men.

Today, it seems barely possible to believe. The international community actually chose to abandon the Tutsi of Rwanda at the very moment when they were being exterminated. Even that was not the end of it. The UN Secretariat officials then instructed General Dallaire that his rump force was not to take an active role in protecting Rwandan citizens. To his great credit, Dallaire manoeuvered to keep the force at almost twice the size authorized, and UNAMIR was still able to save the lives of an estimated 20,000 to 25,000 Rwandans during the course of the genocide.

In a sense, the fact that it was possible to save thousands of lives with 500 troops makes the Belgian and the UN decisions much more deplorable. The available evidence reveals the considerable authority exerted after April 6 by even a small number of Blue Helmets [UN peacekeepers] with a UN flag. [According to political scientist Astri Suhrke] "The general rule" was that "Rwandans were safe as long as they gathered under United Nations protection. . . . It was when the United Nations forces left the site that the killings started." This rule was most infamously demonstrated in the case of the Kigali technical school, l'École Technique Officielle (ETO), where 100 Belgian soldiers kept a horde of murderers at bay. As the UN troops withdrew through one gate, the genocidaires moved in through another. Within hours, the 2,000 Tutsi who had fled to ETO for UN protection were dead. . . .

> Is there a conclusion we can draw . . . other than that expatriate lives were considered more valuable than African lives?

The UN Protected Foreigners, Not Rwandans

With the exception of the deliberate murders of the 10 Belgian Blue Helmets, experiences showed that a few UN troops could provide significant defence for those under their protection with little risk to themselves. This "power of presence" was not to be underestimated. Yet when France sent 500 soldiers to evacuate French citizens . . .

on April 8 and 9, Dallaire's UN troops were immediately ordered—by the Secretariat in New York, and under strong pressure from western countries—to work with the French to evacuate foreign nationals rather than protect threatened Rwandans. This can only be described as a truly perverse use of scarce UN resources. No doubt innocent expatriates were threatened by a conflagration that was none of their making. But exactly the same was true of Rwanda's Tutsi, abandoned by the Blue Helmets.

Equally startling were the guidelines Dallaire was given. These seem to have received little notice until documented by the Carlsson Inquiry report, yet they seem to us of extraordinary significance. "You should make every effort not to compromise your impartiality or to act beyond your mandate," the April 9 cable from Kofi Annan and Iqbal Riza stated, "but [you] may exercise your discretion to do [so] should this be essential for the evacuation of foreign nationals. This should not, repeat not, extend to participating in possible combat except in self-defence." This double standard seems to us outrageous. No such instructions were ever given to Dallaire about protecting innocent Rwandan civilians. He was never explicitly directed that the Blue Helmets should protect such civilians and could fight in self-defence if attacked while doing so. He was never told, "exercise your discretion . . . to act beyond your mandate" when it came to Rwandans. On the contrary, every time he raised the issue, he was specifically instructed not to go beyond the rigidly circumscribed mandate approved by the Security Council under any circumstances. Is there a conclusion we can draw from this incident other than that expatriate lives were considered more valuable than African lives?

The lesson to be learned from the betrayal at ETO and other experiences was that the full potential of UNAMIR went unexplored and unused, and, as a result, countless more Rwandans died than otherwise might have. If anyone in the international community learned this lesson at the time, it was not evident at the UN. For the next six weeks, as the carnage continued, the UN dithered in organizing any kind of response to the ongoing tragedy. The Americans, led by US Ambassador Madeleine Albright, played the key role in blocking more expeditious action by the UN. On May 17, the Security Council finally authorized an expanded UNAMIR II to consist of 5,500 personnel. But there is perhaps no distance greater on earth than the one between the Security Council chambers and the outside world. Once the decision to expand was finally made, . . . the Pentagon somehow required an additional seven weeks just to negotiate a contract for delivering armed personnel carriers to the field; evidently it proved difficult to arrange the desired terms for "maintenance and spare parts." When the genocide ended in mid-July with the final RPF victory, not a single additional UN soldier had landed in Kigali.

Rwandans Coexisted Warily While Awaiting Justice After the Genocide

Elizabeth Neuffer

In the following selection, Elizabeth Neuffer explains that outwardly Rwandans were back to normal behavior within two years of the genocide. But below the surface, powerful emotions seethed. As the population waited for justice to begin, tens of thousands of people remained in jails, while killers returned from exile to walk freely among neighborhoods they had decimated. The government struggled to devise a method to identify, try, and punish those responsible for such a widespread, devastating occurrence. According to Neuffer, no one seemed able to deal conclusively with the aftermath of what the deputy justice minister described as collective insanity. Neuffer's 13-year

SOURCE. Elizabeth Neuffer, *The Key to My Neighbor's House: Seeking Justice in Bosnia and Rwanda*. Basingstoke, Hampshire: United Kingdom, Picador USA, 2001. Copyright © 2001 by Elizabeth Neuffer. All rights reserved. Reproduced with permission of Bloomsbury Publishing PLC and the author.

career as a foreign correspondent for the *Boston Globe* ended when she was killed in a 2003 automobile accident in Iraq, where she had been reporting on the conflicts before and after the U.S. invasion. She previously covered the collapse of the Soviet Union, the Balkan wars of the 1990s, and the aftermath of the Rwandan genocide.

What first surprised me was Rwanda's seeming normality. Unlike Bosnia, which in some ways resembled London after the Blitz, Rwanda was largely unscathed physically after the fighting of 1994. Only the bullet holes that pockmarked the side of the Parliament building in the capital, Kigali, bore witness to recent clashes. The rest of the city seemed peaceful: purple and pink bougainvillea along the roadside, gaily painted storefronts, villas with balconies perched on the hill, tall acacia and cypress trees.

And then there were all the people—crowds of people—streaming along the road with baskets of food perched on their heads, jamming the outdoor markets, strolling the streets. I had expected the streets to be desolate, the markets empty, because between 500,000 and 1 million people had perished and hundreds of thousands more had decamped to Zaire. I had thought I would have been able to see the legacy of the genocide in the absence of Rwandans themselves.

Yet Rwanda had been overpopulated to begin with, and after the RPF [Rwandan Patriotic Front, a Tutsi-led force] victory, some 750,000 Tutsi who had lived in Uganda or other African countries since 1959 had finally returned home with their families. They returned with a burning sense of justice, a desire to improve the land, but almost no knowledge of its customs, practices, or even its official language, French, much less its native

> 'This is the land of the walking dead.'

language, Kinyarwandan. They spoke English, the language used in Uganda.

As a result of the influx, the country was oddly trifurcated. There were Tutsi survivors of the genocide, crippled, impoverished, and poor. There were returning Tutsi, more modern, more European, better off, who knew of genocide only from news accounts. And then there were the country's many Hutu—its majority—a mixture of those who had nothing to do with the genocide, those who were victimized by it, and those who took part in it.

People Concealed Post-Genocide Emotions

At first, Rwanda's seeming normalcy made the pain and loss wrought by the genocide almost impossible to grasp. The restaurants were open, the banks in operation, and bustling markets offered everything from women's shoes to black-market foreign currency. It took me some weeks to realize that the legacy of Rwanda's genocide lived on in people's inner lives. Survivors, whether Tutsi or Hutu, went through the motions of everyday existence but not its emotions; they skated across their feelings, frightened of experiencing them too deeply. One of my translators, Françoise—whose family had been killed in the genocide—answered me this way when I asked her how the slaughter had affected Rwandan society. "Look right in front of you," she replied. "We have all lost something. We even have an expression for it: *bapfuye buhagazi*. It means the walking dead. This is the land of the walking dead."

During the weeks and months I spent in Rwanda, I came to absorb what she meant. The people I befriended understood intellectually what had happened to them: they had lost their entire family or their homes, or they had been raped or had narrowly escaped death. But they were not yet reconciled with those losses. The speed with

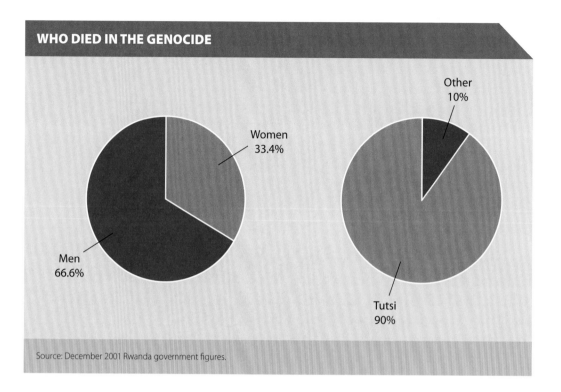

WHO DIED IN THE GENOCIDE

Women
33.4%

Men
66.6%

Other
10%

Tutsi
90%

Source: December 2001 Rwanda government figures.

which the genocide took place—the killing lasted just 100 days—had deprived victims of the time to come to terms with it. So did the reality of living in Rwanda, as Tutsi and Hutu coexisted in an uneasy truce. Everyone I met had a family member who was either a victim of the genocide or accused of taking part in it. Rwandans, deeply private by nature, had become even more so; they didn't trust their neighbors, their friends, their family, or themselves. Conversations had the strained air of a Victorian-era tea party, at which emotions were never mentioned.

Who could live with such fear, suspicions, and anguish, day in and day out? No wonder people seemed to be sleepwalking through life. All that kept them together, other than deep ties to the land, was the promise of the future: the promise made by the RPF government that Rwanda would be for all Rwandans and would deliver an even-handed justice. Authorities vowed to follow the terms set down by the Arusha accords, which established power-sharing between the Hutu and Tutsi and different political parties. At first the Tutsi-led RPF tried to be all-inclusive: Of twenty-two government ministers, sixteen were Hutu and just five from the RPF. Symbolically, Rwanda's president was Hutu: Pasteur Bizimungu, one of the Hutu who had sided with the RPF before their invasion.

An Uneasy Alliance

Yet the real power broker was the swashbuckling General Paul Kagame, the man behind the 1990 RPF invasion that preceded the genocide. The government in reality was an uneasy alliance of conqueror and conquered that, by 1996, had all but fallen apart. Hutu officials, finding themselves disenfranchised by Kagame and his supporters, quit in disgust, claiming the RPF government was not one of national unity after all. First to go was the Hutu chief of staff, J.D. Ntakirutimana. He was followed by the Hutu prime minister, Faustin Twagiramungu. "Some of us believed the RPF victory would enable us to achieve real change," Twagiramungu said. "But the RPF has simply installed a new form of Tutsi power." Four others resigned and left the country shortly afterward, including Interior Minister Seth Sendashonga, a well-respected moderate, critical of what he believed to be reprisal killings of civilians by the RPF army.

While Hutu still dominated the Rwandan cabinet in 1996, their presence was more token than influential. The Tutsi, particularly those returning from Uganda, held the real power and dominated all other political, judicial, intellectual, and even economic institutions in the country. In every town I went to, the mayor, or burgomaster, was Tutsi, regardless of the area's ethnic mix. Consequently, the country's Hutu felt disenfranchised, particularly because Hutu were still being indiscriminately accused of war crimes, arrested and jailed. Reprisals for the genocide were common: The country's army, the RPA, once a highly disciplined force, had picked up new Tutsi recruits who reveled in violence and used their newfound power to harass and kill Hutu. Twagiramungu estimated that as many as 310,000 Hutu had been killed.

By November 1996, Rwanda's strained peace faced a new challenge when events brewing across the border in Zaire finally bubbled over. The tens of thousands of Rwandan Hutu in the refugee camps were on the move. While many had fled westward—away from Rwanda—many more, coming under attack from Zairean Tutsi rebels, had turned to flee eastward, toward Rwanda. After two years, they were headed home.

> So determined were the Hutu returnees that they crossed the border at the rate of nearly 200 people per minute.

A Hutu Multitude Returned

The first trickle of returning refugees—carrying battered leather suitcases and balancing dirty bedrolls on their heads—washed over the Rwandan border on November 11. As I stood by the metal gate manned on both sides by surly bureaucrats wielding rubber stamps with abandon, the refugees limped across, exhausted. The returning Rwandan Hutu told of hunger, of wandering for weeks in the jungle, of being attacked by Zairean Tutsi rebels. "I saw so many dead bodies I stopped counting," Devota Mukarusema, a mother of six, told me as she leaned on her wooden staff by the roadside, tears mingling with the sweat coursing down her face.

By November 15, however, that trickle had swollen to a flood, and standing at the border was like watching an angry river's swift, inexorable currents breach a breakwater. Tens of thousands of people were marching home. The undulating column of returning Hutu was

nearly twenty-five miles long, moving and shimmering under the sun, and no matter how high a hill one climbed, it still stretched from one horizon to another. On and on and on they came, calabashes and plastic jugs of water on their heads, babies on their backs, bags of food in their arms, walking with bare feet or, in the case of one woman, in one golden slipper. So determined were the Hutu returnees that they crossed the border at the rate of nearly 200 people per minute. By midday a transit camp near the Rwandan border designed to hold 30,000 refugees was already full. All along the road from Zaire into Rwanda, the air smelled of pungent sweat and sweet eucalyptus. Families, tired after what had often proven to be a march of several weeks, camped out by the roadside and lighted brush fires.

> That morning [a Tutsi woman] had seen the faces of two men she thought she would only see again in her nightmares: two members of the Hutu militia who had slaughtered her neighbors.

And yet they continued, hips and heads and shoulders swaying, men and women and grandmothers and adolescents and children and crying babies. Some pregnant women, swept up in the return, gave birth on the road. "No, there is no name yet," said Elisabeth Nyiranfubakuze, holding up a corner of the *pagne* [fabric] she had wrapped around herself, to show her newborn baby's wrinkled face. "I am just too tired."

To the surprise of Western aid officials, scurrying to set up makeshift camps and organize the distribution of humanitarian aid, many of the returning refugees looked the picture of health, carrying plenty of provisions with them for their march. Indeed, their return looked less like an urgent flight from armed rebels than a planned evacuation. "They're carrying firewood—how many people fleeing for their lives carry firewood?" wondered Russell Nielson of Save the Children Foundation, as he

Photo on previous page: By 1996, Paul Kagame, who commanded the Tutsi-led Rwandan Patriotic Front in the civil war, was Rwanda's key power broker, and able to shape the national mood. (Alexander Joe/ AFP/Getty Images.)

tried to wind his truck through the packed crowd at the Rwandan border.

Fearful People Heard a Promise for Peace

That night I found myself struggling for ways to describe what I had witnessed, this mass movement of people. The flow had not abated by nightfall, and indeed it would take four days for all the refugees to cross. At a loss, I settled for the word "exodus" to describe the return of the Hutu in the story I wrote for the *Boston Globe*, even though the expression was a cliché. In retrospect, it was not such a bad choice, for it is in Exodus—the second book of the Old Testament—that questions of sin, justice, and forgiveness are first raised in the Bible. God is enraged when he discovers the people of Israel have made a golden calf to worship, despite his orders not to make any graven image. Moses pleads for forgiveness on their behalf. God, in turn, defines justice: "The Lord . . . forgiving iniquity and transgression and sin, but who will by no means clear the guilty. . . . "

Understanding evil, defining repentance, avoiding vengeance, delivering judgment, granting forgiveness: These were the issues three-quarters of a million returning Hutu now posed for Rwanda. Indeed, they were issues the country was already meeting head-on. That afternoon, President Bizimungu had climbed on top of a pile of potato sacks at the border and greeted the refugees through a bullhorn. "Your brothers are waiting for you in Rwanda," he bellowed. "Together we will build a new Rwanda where peace will prevail. Do not be afraid."

Unofficially, feelings were anything but hopeful. In tiny villages near the border, where Tutsi had been killed with a vengeance, small groups of survivors greeted the news of the Hutu return with as much enthusiasm as a death warrant. Nyundo, a small village that crept up a lush hillside some twenty miles from the border, was one such place. Its white cathedral, the largest building for miles, was where almost 500 Tutsi, including some 30 Catholic priests, were massacred in 1994. Outside the cathedral's wooden door a hand-painted sign read: "We must pray that those who committed genocide never return to their country. To kill is against God's words."

I found Suzanne Nyirantagorama sitting underneath that sign the day after the first Hutu returned. She had been crouched there for some hours, her thin arms encircling knees she had drawn up protectively to her chest. That morning she had seen the faces of two men she thought she would only see again in her nightmares: two members of the Hutu militia who had slaughtered her neighbors but somehow, in their frenzy, had missed Suzanne and her family. They had just returned to Nyundo. Had they come there for her, now one of only ten surviving Tutsi in the village? "I am frightened," she said, putting her head down on her knees, as if she could curl into a ball and simply disappear from sight. "I don't know if they came back with a good heart or if they will continue their killing."

Father Jean-Marie Vianney Nsengumuremyi, Nyundo cathedral's priest and also a massacre survivor, strode out of the church, his green-and-white cape billowing. We stood on the cathedral steps and looked down on the road below, where the endless line of returning refugees marched past the smoke of roadside campfires. He shook his head. How easy it would be for Rwanda to erupt into violence again, for hatred to persist, for vengeance to take hold. "Justice must work here," he said firmly, as if to remind himself to add it to his prayers. "Without it, we can't advance."

Friends, Relatives, and Killers Returned

Later that day I again returned to the border crossing just outside the graceful city of Gisenyi. As I scanned the crowd of returning Hutu, I wondered just who was whom and what role each had played in the genocide. What about that man in the pink shorts and red shirt, a yellow jerry can strapped to his hip, his well-muscled shoulders barely straining under the sack balanced on his head? Was he responsible for the killing at Nyundo? Or that teenager there, with the green windbreaker and the blue flip-flops, or even that woman, her purple-and-white *pagnes* wrapped around her, a bedroll on her head. What had they done?

> 'What would you do if you saw those responsible for killing your family?'

I was not alone in scrutinizing the tired, lined faces of the refugees marching home. Crowds of Tutsi and Hutu stood at the border, looking for enemies as well as friends and relatives. My translator, Françoise, broke into my thoughts as we stood there. All eight of her family had been slaughtered by Hutu militia in Gisenyi; she lived simply because she'd been at a neighbor's house when the killers arrived. Survivors' guilt was a burden she, a staunch Catholic who found solace in her faith, bore without complaint.

"See that one?" Françoise said, pointing to a small man shuffling along, bowed under the weight of his suitcase on his back. "I'm pretty sure he's the man who killed my neighbor up the street." She strained forward to look. "Yes, that's him." She nodded.

Françoise had told me earlier that she had a good idea of who had killed her family. So I asked, "What would you do if you saw those responsible for killing your family?"

"I've been looking at the crowd," she said, continuing to peer at the faces parading by. "So far I haven't seen anyone responsible for my family's death."

I persisted. "But what if you did?"

Françoise sighed. Conflicting emotions played across her broad face. She was quiet for a good five minutes, searching her soul, asking her God for guidance.

"Vengeance," she said finally, "won't bring my family back. The answer lies in justice and in God."

Rwandans See a Hugely Flawed Tribunal

Who was to deliver this justice? The International Criminal Tribunal for Rwanda was to prosecute the key leaders of the genocide, but most Rwandans had swiftly dismissed it as ineffective. For one thing, it promised an unequal justice. The Rwanda Tribunal intended to judge the genocide's most heinous criminals; yet the most severe penalty one could receive from the court was life imprisonment. That meant that the high-ranking architects of mass murder would receive a more lenient sentence than the smaller fry judged by Rwanda's own courts, which routinely handed down the death sentence. This seeming irrationality made little sense to anyone.

And the tribunal, Rwandans were swift to point out, still had yet to do anything. Twenty-one indictments had been issued and thirteen people were in custody. Yet nearly two years after the court's founding, trials had not yet begun. It was as if the United Nations and its member states had drawn no lessons from their peacekeeping mission in Rwanda, where under-equipped and outnumbered soldiers watched helplessly as the genocide commenced, their cries for reinforcements ignored. The Rwanda Tribunal also had little funding. Like its sister tribunal in The Hague, it received money only on a stopgap basis, making it impossible to recruit staff. In January, the UN Special Rapporteur on Rwanda had appealed to the UN to "increase the budget of the International Tribunal in order to provide it with the necessary human and material means to fulfil its mission as effectively as possible." Still, the Rwanda Tribunal received only $36 million in 1996, doled out

> Rwanda's justice system, which had suffered for decades from the whims of its various rulers, was partisan and corrupt.

in three-month increments, and the slow-moving UN bureaucracy was slow to respond to the court's needs.

The shortfall was obvious on the ground. Tribunal investigators arrived in Gisenyi, anxious to cross into Zaire and check the now-abandoned camps for incriminating evidence left behind by Hutu leaders. But no one had approved their travel orders and they couldn't enter Zaire without them. They were reduced to hanging around the hotel pool, pouncing on journalists who might have documents they could use. "You just back from Zaire? Did you make it to Mugunga [a refugee camp]? Did you find anything?" asked one tribunal investigator, as I arrived back late one evening clasping papers in my arms.

In the absence of an effective tribunal, Rwanda was left to itself to dispense justice. Justice was one of the RPF government's bywords and reforming the justice system one of their top priorities. But these goals would be difficult to achieve. Rwanda's justice system, which had suffered for decades from the whims of its various rulers, was partisan and corrupt. No independent association of defense attorneys had existed, just one appointed by the government, and its lawyers frequently lacked legal training. After the genocide, little remained of the country's judicial system. The majority of lawyers and staff had been killed. Out of 750 judges, only 244 had survived. Courtrooms and offices were smashed, furniture and equipment stolen or destroyed. The windows of the Ministry of Justice building in Kigali had been blown out and its case files set afire. Law books had vanished as had copies of the country's code of criminal procedure.

In the absence of a functioning police and judiciary, Rwanda's army was making sweeping arrests, in theory, to ensure people did not take vengeance into their own hands. The country's prisons were filled to overflowing. But Rwandan justice, human rights groups warned, was far from even-handed. Some 80,000 Rwandans, nearly all Hutu, were behind bars. There were rarely case files explaining why someone had been arrested. Those being trained to fill the jobs of judges and prosecutors were almost all Tutsi, hardly a reflection of the country's ethnic mix. Now some 750,000 Hutu Rwandans—many implicated in the genocide—were on their way home. Who would judge them?

At the Ministry of Justice, Deputy Justice Minister Gerald Gahima had been assigned to bring the country's justice system up to speed. A tall man, thin as a drinking straw, Gahima was a Tutsi who had grown up in Uganda. An optimist about what Rwanda could accomplish, he noted with pride how far the country had progressed in a mere two years. With Western aid, the government had rebuilt courthouses, including the Supreme Court.

It had installed a few telephones, collected law books, and begun training a handful of new judges and prosecutors. Some $44.6 million had been pledged to overhaul the justice system, although about $66 million was needed.

> Prisoners had been fingered by a neighbor jealous of his property or eager to settle scores.

Still, Gahima admitted, because of the mass nature of the crimes, justice would mean distinguishing not only between good and bad but also between innumerable shades of gray. "The crimes committed here involve everyone," he told me. "If a million people died, then you have to figure at least 2 to 3 million are complicit in the crimes. But you can't prosecute them all. We must punish the leaders and find a way of dealing more leniently with the rest."

Parliament Establishes Levels of Guilt

Agreeing how to do that was proving no easy task. Questions of justice divided the government. Its moderates, both Tutsi and Hutu, wanted only the most high-ranking, powerful participants in the genocide to be prosecuted, hoping to spur their country toward reconciliation. But RPF hard-liners wanted as many of the guilty people to be arrested and punished as possible.

It took months of heated debate before Rwanda's Parliament passed the country's genocide law in August 1996, a law that was actually more lenient than many desired. The law divided crimes into categories with different penalties, ranging from Category 1, the architects and planners of the genocide who would receive the death penalty, down to Category 4, or those involved with property crimes. Quite controversially, it allowed for defendants in Categories 3 and 4 to plea-bargain after a confession and an apology. The hope was that scores of the accused—dubbed *génocidaires*—would confess, emptying the prisons and clearing the docket so trials would move swiftly when they began in 1997.

Up in the hills, people were already publicizing the government's new law, hoping returnees would sign up to confess. I'd seen them there, using a megaphone to summon residents scattered in homes along the hillside, and then trying to explain the concept to them. I asked Gahima about those returning from Zaire. How did the government plan to ensure that suspected killers weren't the target of vengeance, rather than justice, when they moved back home? Gahima acknowledged the question with a nod. For now, the plan was to arrest only Category 1 offenders, the leaders, he explained. (Despite good intentions, however, an estimated 6,810 returnees were arrested by mid-January 1997.)

But what about those already in jail? I asked. How long would they have to wait for trials? What if innocent people had been put behind bars accidentally in the first wave of arrests? Both Rwandan and Western human rights groups were finding cases in which prisoners had been fingered by a neighbor jealous of his property or eager to settle scores. If the Rwandan government was trying to send a message that impunity was over and a new era of justice had begun, shouldn't the justice system have to meet the highest possible standards?

Silence. Then Gahima looked at me. "The problem isn't just one human being committing a crime against another," he replied. "But all human beings were doing things that no one could imagine a human could do. It was as if there was a kind of collective insanity. . . . " His voice trailed off.

"What you end up with in a post-genocide society is not justice," the deputy justice minister concluded. Perhaps we should think of another word for it."

CHAPTER 2

Controversies Surrounding the Rwandan Genocide

The World's Indifference Allowed Mass Murder

Milton Leitenberg

In the following viewpoint, Milton Leitenberg asserts that with the U.S. government determined to remain uninvolved, other countries as well as the United Nations did very little to prevent or diminish the 1994 genocide in Rwanda. The UN had a small force in Rwanda when the killing began, and its charter clearly permitted the use of troops to save lives, Leitenberg explains, but instead the UN response was to withdraw. Even the Organization of African Unity failed to intervene. Leitenberg, author and senior research scholar at the University of Maryland, is known for his work regarding arms control, conflict studies, biological weaponry, and international interventions.

SOURCE. Milton Leitenberg, "Rwanda, 1994: International Incompetence Produces Genocide," *Peacekeeping & International Relations*, vol. 23, November-December 1994, pp. 6–10. Copyright © 1994 Peacekeeping & International Relations, property of Canadian Peacekeeping Press. Reproduced by permission of the author.

On April 6, 1994, the Presidents of Burundi and Rwanda were both returning to the Rwandan capital of Kigali from a UN-mediated parley of the contending parties of both countries with other regional leaders. The Rwandan president was under strong international pressure once again, this time to implement the 1993 peace agreement. The airplane in which the leaders were travelling was shot down as it approached the Kigali airport. In less than an hour, road-side barriers began to go up in the Rwandan capital, and the killings began, carried out at first by the Presidential Guard. It was not a spontaneous outbreak of violence; it had clearly been planned. Among the first victims were not only Tutsi, but members of the Hutu political opposition. The killings were at first confined to the capital, but the response of the United States and other Western countries was only to evacuate their own nationals in great haste. Presented with this Western "hands off" reaction, a major role in the massacres was passed on to the militias, which fanned out into the government-controlled portion of the country with the aid of the military.

Under the terms of the peace accord, the United Nations Assistance Mission to Rwanda (UNAMIR)—a 2,500-member UN observer force—was present in Rwanda at the time, without Chapter VII provisions to use force. Article 42 in Chapter VII of the United Nations Charter provides for the use of force: ". . . such action as may be necessary . . ." in any circumstance of "threat to the peace, breach of peace, or act of aggression." It provides for the use of "all necessary means," the diplomatic phrase which means the use of force. The UN had authorized such use sparingly in the post-war years: in the Korean war, in the Congo, for the U.S.-led coalition that fought Iraq after its invasion of Kuwait in 1990, in UN resolution 794 for the U.S.-led coalition that went to Somalia in December 1992, as well as for the

UN forces that replaced it. Force is also authorized for certain missions to which UN forces have been assigned in Yugoslavia, although for the most part it has not been applied there. On April 5, one day before the violence broke out in Kigali, the UN Security Council had extended UNAMIR's mandate for six weeks, but threatened to end it unless "... full and prompt implementation by the parties . . . of the transitional institutions provided for under the Arusha Peace Agreements . . ." took place.

A week after the killing began, estimates of those massacred reached 20,000, then 50,000. At some point very soon after they began, General Romeo Dallaire, the Canadian commander of UNAMIR, requested the Office of the UN Secretary-General to provide him with new Rules of Engagement for his forces so that he could protect innocent civilians. The request was rejected. In mid-April, Belgium decided to recall the 440 troops that it had serving with the UNAMIR force after ten of its disarmed soldiers had been murdered on April 7 by members of the Presidential Guard, who also assassinated a government minister whom the troops were protecting. After that, the remaining UN troops stayed in their barracks. UN Secretary-General Boutros Boutros-Ghali, with the support of the U.S. administration, essentially recommended to the Security Council that the entire remaining UNAMIR force be withdrawn. He noted that with the withdrawal of the Belgian contingent, UNAMIR would be unable to carry out its mandate, and stated that, "In these circumstances, I have asked my Special Representative and the Force Commander to prepare plans for the withdrawal of UNAMIR, should this prove necessary." In the end, such a retreat was considered to be too great an embarrassment, and the Security Council allowed 270 troops to remain.

> The major reason for Security Council inaction was the criticism and opposition by the United States.

The Organization of African Unity [OAU] criticized the UN's decision to withdraw all but a symbolic and non-functional presence as "a sign of indifference or lack of sufficient concern" for Africans. Yet in a pattern of response typical of the OAU, once killings begin in an African state, not a single African country sent new or additional troops to Rwanda, except for the Senegalese unit that would later join the much-criticized French forces when these were deployed in June.

Other Nations Talk But Do Not Act

By April 29, three weeks after the killing had started, Mr. Boutros-Ghali reported that as many as 200,000 people had been killed—massacred—in Rwanda. By now having reversed his earlier recommendation to withdraw the peacekeeping troops, he proposed three options, the first of which was again prompted by General Dallaire, and called for Security Council approval of a plan to send in 5,550 additional troops.

It was understood by all that it would take months for the troops to be raised from member nations, equipped and actually deployed. Again, Security Council members from African countries and other developing nations favoured forceful action. But the U.S. opposed this option, no African nation actually volunteered troops, and the Security Council asked the Secretary-General to "consult" with the OAU and to undertake new "diplomatic steps." As could be expected, the now-desperate diplomatic appeals from the Secretary-General to the parties to the conflict produced nothing.

The major reason for Security Council inaction was the criticism and opposition by the United States. Rwanda became the first application of President [Bill] Clinton's admonition in an address to the United Nations on September 27, 1993, that the UN must learn "when to say no." The UN needed to ask "hard questions" before sending peacekeeping forces to any additional sites,

The UN Chief Looks Back

On a speaking tour of Africa in 1998, United Nations secretary-general Kofi Annan told the Rwandan parliament that "we will not deny that, in their greatest hour of need, the world failed the people of Rwanda."

Annan, who was UN under-secretary for peacekeeping in 1994 when the genocide took place, said: "The international community and the United Nations could not muster the political will to confront it. The world must deeply repent this failure."

He pledged UN support for Rwandan peace and progress, but said only the Rwandan people could end violence within the country.

and it must recognize that it "cannot become engaged in every one of the world's conflicts." The United States would only agree to a UN resolution that authorized sending a new force after Secretary-General Boutros-Ghali had reported back on various conditions adapted from those recently established for itself by the U.S. administration, some of which are patently unachievable in the real world, or cannot be realistically determined in advance. Presidential Decision Directive 25 (PDD-25) was formally issued in May 1994, and listed seven factors that the U.S. government would consider if required to vote on peace operations in the UN Security Council, six additional and more stringent factors to consider if the participation of U.S. forces was involved, and three final factors if the U.S. forces might be engaged in combat—16 considerations in all. The document (drafting of which originally began in February 1993 as PD-13) underwent a most extraordinary evolution from U.S. Ambassador Madeleine Albright's statement of June 1993 on "assertive multilateralism." As a result of the casualties suffered by U.S. forces in Somalia, it became a policy of stringent conditionality.

The great likelihood is that these conditions will most often be used to rationalize inaction, which is unquestionably their effect to date. *New York Times* editorials applauded the U.S. "prudence." Although she was not herself altogether in agreement with the administration's Rwanda policy, Ambassador Albright presented a disingenuous defense of the U.S. opposition in a television performance on May 19, claiming that the U.S. was only "trying to help" the UN by calling for delay and reexamination. A secondary U.S. consideration was the 30 percent of the UN peacekeeping costs that the U.S. would have to bear for any new peacekeeping deployment while the U.S. was already grossly in arrears for past assessments.

> 'We cannot dispatch our troops to solve every problem where our values are offended by human misery, and we should not.'

Troops Are Recommended But Not Dispatched

On May 11, the Secretary-General formally asked that the plan be approved, and on May 17, a Security Council resolution was finally passed. By this time, senior aid officials in Rwanda were quoting a figure of half a million dead. On May 25, Secretary-General Boutros-Ghali announced his defeat and failure in attempting to raise contributions of military forces from UN member nations. During all these weeks, the U.S. government had also instructed its spokesmen "not to describe the deaths there as genocide, even though some senior officials believe that is exactly what they represent." Obviously, had U.S. administration spokesmen openly referred to "genocide," it would have been more difficult simply to stand aside and watch the slaughter continue. Two days later, on May 27, President Clinton met with the UN

Secretary-General and declined to commit any U.S. forces to Rwanda. In a Memorial Day address to the American public, Clinton stated, ". . . we cannot dispatch our troops to solve every problem where our values are offended by human misery, and we should not." He repeated the

The Organization of African Unity—addressed in this picture by Libyan leader Moammar Gadhafi in 2002—was one of several international organizations that failed to intervene in the Rwandan genocide. (**AP Images.**)

same sentiments almost verbatim in a second Memorial [Day] weekend address at the U.S. Naval Academy: "We cannot solve every such outburst of civil strife or militant nationalism simply by sending in our forces."

On June 3, the leaders of 14 African states, stung by the UN Secretary-General's description of the situation as "a scandal," offered to send troop contingents—at some indeterminate time, after they were armed and equipped to a certain standard. (Among their requests was one for 200 artillery pieces for a contingent of 1,000 men.) On its side, the U.S. Department of Defense consumed weeks in disputing with the UN the level of repayment that it should receive for supplying 50 armored personnel carriers. In mid-June it was still demanding that it be reimbursed $15 million for the shipping costs to and from Rwanda, spare parts, etc. Estimates of those dead had now reached 500,000, even 800,000. The 50 U.S. vehicles did not arrive until mid-July.

On July 20, with a cholera epidemic spreading among a portion of the Hutu refugees who had fled following the victory of the Rwandan Patriotic Front (fearing retribution for the months of slaughtering Tutsi and other Hutus), USAID [United States Agency for International Development] Administrator Brian Atwood recommended that the UN dispatch a large peacekeeping force. President Clinton asked for $320 million of emergency relief funds, and, on July 22, suggested sending 4,000 U.S. troops. The *New York Times* editorial headline was "At Last, Rwanda's Pain Registers." All of this four months after the troops and money could have prevented the catastrophe in the first place.

Nevertheless, U.S. officials from the President on down remained adamant that the U.S. military forces deployed to the area would be engaged only in humanitarian relief activities and would not do any "peacekeeping." U.S. Secretary of Defense [William] Perry explained that the United States military had unique capabilities for airlift and logistics—but not for peacekeeping: "It would not be the best use of our forces." Four days later, while visiting the refugee camp in Goma, Zaire, Perry explained that, "The United States does not have combat forces here, therefore we are not providing peacekeeping." Obviously the combat forces were not there because they had not been ordered to be there by the President or by Secretary of Defense Perry. At the very moment that Perry was speaking, 2,000 first-line U.S. Marine and Army personnel had been ordered to fight forest fires in Washington state. The armed forces of the United States, the world's most thoroughly equipped, trained, and ready military force, was suddenly incapable of performing peacekeeping duties, and was only uniquely capable of logistics.

As of September, the U.S. Senate was willing to authorize only $170 million of the $320 million that President Clinton had asked for. In addition, the Senate wrote into the legislation the provision that all U.S. forces had to be withdrawn from Rwanda by October 1 unless Congress specifically approved a longer stay. As the U.S. troops began to be withdrawn from the area, it became known that the Department of Defense had decided not to carry out some of the four tasks that the U.S. administration had publicly announced that it would assume on behalf of the United Nations and the UN High Commissioner for Refugees. As for the Mobutu government in Zaire, it did nothing to disarm the 40,000 soldiers of the former Hutu government's army who were on its territory and in the larger refugee camps in Zaire, and who were actively preventing Hutu refugees from returning to Rwanda. Incomparable national and international irresponsibility and incompetence was stubbornly maintained to the very last moment.

> Two sides warring for supreme power or one or more of them slaughtering its own population will not suddenly agree to issue polite invitations to UN or other forces.

Conditions Should Have Triggered Response

This case provides a classic example of the requirement for automatic thresholds of civilian casualties that would compel the rapid deployment of United Nations or other large multinational forces. There are two circumstances in which this should be considered mandatory. The first is massive massacre of civilian populations, exactly as was occurring in Rwanda, and as had previously occurred in both Rwanda and Burundi between the same two ethnic groups. The second circumstance is evidence of premeditated actions that lead to large-scale civilian starvation during war or armed conflict. There have been some 16 events since 1945 in which these conditions have been met, with mortalities in these events ranging from around 100,000 to around 1.5 million, and a cumulative mortality of over 11 million people. Many of these have occurred in Africa: Burundi, Somalia, Ethiopia, Sudan, Uganda, Angola, Mozambique, and Rwanda. It is also interesting to note that there are a substantial number of repeat offenders among these. It is inconceivable that any international body would set such thresholds above 50,000 dead human beings, if that high. In the Rwanda case, such numbers were reached in a matter of a few weeks.

And it is obvious that such deployment would have to be under Chapter VII provisions of the United Nations Charter, with the mandate to use deadly force without waiting for the approval or tolerance of the combatants, or of a governing perpetrator. Two sides warring for supreme power or one or more of them slaughtering its own population will not suddenly agree to issue polite invitations to UN or other forces. In Rwanda, both the government carrying out the genocidal massacres and the Rwandan Patriotic Front fighting to seize political power rejected suggestions of a UN intervention force. The latter feared that a UN presence would maintain the status quo, with the government continuing to hold power in the capital. Astonishing as it may also seem to outside observers, the contending parties in Burundi at present—military leaders and leaders of political factions—rejected a United Nations proposal in mid-August [1994] to deploy a peacekeeping force with observer and monitoring functions, despite witnessing the carnage between their ethnic brethren directly across the border in Rwanda.

All of this is nevertheless far from consideration by any UN member state or international body. The UNAMIR forces that were in Rwanda when the killings started should have been immediately reinforced by substantial deployments from additional states. And the UN Security Council quickly should have provided the authorization for UNAMIR to use force. Nations that feared France's motive for sending peacekeeping troops to Rwanda later in June could have resolved such doubts best by joining the force in contingents of equal size. The French forces were notably deployed with explicit and well-announced orders to fire upon anyone who threatened or attacked civilians in their area, or their own forces. It is inconceivable that any nation, not to speak of a great power, should panic and withdraw its forces on taking a small number of casualties, as was the response of the U.S. administration and of members of Congress following the events in Somalia. Other nations took casualties in Somalia earlier, and have done so since those suffered by the U.S. forces. Until the great powers in the UN Security Council are willing to act together, and to absorb a comparatively small number of casualties to prevent massive mortality, there will continue to be after the fact hand-wringing and aid efforts when it is too late.

There is one last point of major importance given the attention that "ethnic" wars and conflicts are getting at the moment. Few if any of these are spontaneous, historically inevitable, or driven by historical grievances. They owe their occurrence to conscious manipulation by senior national political figures or parties, in or out of office, for immediate political purposes at the present time. This was the case for Rwanda and the ruling Hutu party; Serbia ("Yugoslavia") and Slobodan Milosevic; Kenya and the sudden attacks on Kikuyu villagers in the last year or two prompted by President Daniel Arap Moi's party; India and the Bharatiya Janata Party in the events in 1992 and 1993; the war in Sudan; and the possibility of North-South, Hausa, and Fulani versus Yoruba conflict which may yet develop into open fighting in Nigeria. These frequently genocidal conflicts are initiated and prompted by political actors for present political ends.

Between 1948 and 1988, the U.S. Senate would not ratify the UN Convention on Genocide on the rationale that its enforcement might lead to encroachments on national sovereignty. The result of similar logic on the international level is that the world has watched some 15 occasions since 1960 in which several hundred thousand to several million people have massacred each other while no international agency has intervened to stop the slaughter.

The U.S. Government Missed Many Chances to Stop the Killings

Samantha Power

> In the following viewpoint, Samantha Power states that U.S. government officials—even the ones knowledgeable about Rwanda—did nothing to stop the genocide, even as it became undeniable that thousands of people were being slaughtered. The reasons for this inaction included many factors that seemed reasonable to the officials at the time. Power notes that, in spite of extensive media coverage and mounting reports of the widespread killings perpetrated by the Hutu leadership against the Tutsis, the U.S. government did not use the word "genocide" to describe events in Rwanda, hoping to avoid international pressure to intervene. Journalist and professor Samantha Power is the author of *A Problem from Hell: America and the Age of Genocide*, which won the 2003 Pulitzer Prize for general nonfiction.

SOURCE. Samantha Power, "Bystanders to Genocide," *The Atlantic*, vol. 288, September 2001, pp. 84–108. Copyright © 2001 by Samantha Power, used with permission of The Wylie Agency LLC.

In the course of a hundred days in 1994, the Hutu government of Rwanda and its extremist allies very nearly succeeded in exterminating the country's Tutsi minority. Using firearms, machetes, and a variety of garden implements, Hutu militiamen, soldiers, and ordinary citizens murdered some 800,000 Tutsi and politically moderate Hutu. It was the fastest, most efficient killing spree of the twentieth century.

> As the terror in Rwanda had unfolded, [President Bill] Clinton had shown virtually no interest in stopping the genocide.

A few years later, in a series in the *New Yorker*, Philip Gourevitch recounted in horrific detail the story of the genocide and the world's failure to stop it. President Bill Clinton, a famously avid reader, expressed shock. He sent copies of Gourevitch's articles to his second-term national-security adviser, Sandy Berger. The articles bore confused, angry, searching queries in the margins. "Is what he's saying true?" Clinton wrote with a thick black felt-tip pen beside heavily underlined paragraphs. "How did this happen?" he asked, adding, "I want to get to the bottom of this." The President's urgency and outrage were oddly timed. As the terror in Rwanda had unfolded, Clinton had shown virtually no interest in stopping the genocide, and his Administration had stood by as the death toll rose into the hundreds of thousands.

Why did the United States not do more for the Rwandans at the time of the killings? Did the President really not know about the genocide, as his marginalia suggested? Who were the people in his Administration who made the life-and-death decisions that dictated U.S. policy? Why did they decide (or decide not to decide) as they did? Were any voices inside or outside the U.S. government demanding that the United States do more? If so, why weren't they heeded? And most crucial, what could the United States have done to save lives?

So far people have explained the U.S. failure to respond to the Rwandan genocide by claiming that the United States didn't know what was happening, that it knew but didn't care, or that regardless of what it knew there was nothing useful to be done. The account that follows is based on a three-year investigation involving sixty interviews with senior, mid-level, and junior State Department, Defense Department, and National Security Council officials who helped to shape or inform U.S. policy. It also reflects dozens of interviews with Rwandan, European, and United Nations officials and with peacekeepers, journalists, and nongovernmental workers in Rwanda. Thanks to the National Security Archive, a nonprofit organization that uses the Freedom of Information Act to secure the release of classified U.S. documents, this account also draws on hundreds of pages of newly available government records. This material provides a clearer picture than was previously possible of the interplay among people, motives, and events. It reveals that the U.S. government knew enough about the genocide early on to save lives, but passed up countless opportunities to intervene.

Later, Clinton Spoke of the Terror

In March of 1998, on a visit to Rwanda, President Clinton issued what would later be known as the "Clinton apology," which was actually a carefully hedged acknowledgment. He spoke to the crowd assembled on the tarmac at Kigali Airport: "We come here today partly in recognition of the fact that we in the United States and the world community did not do as much as we could have and should have done to try to limit what occurred" in Rwanda.

This implied that the United States had done a good deal but not quite enough. In reality, the United States did much more than fail to send troops. It led a successful effort to remove most of the UN peacekeepers who

were already in Rwanda. It aggressively worked to block the subsequent authorization of UN reinforcements. It refused to use its technology to jam radio broadcasts that were a crucial instrument in the coordination and perpetuation of the genocide. And even as, on average, 8,000 Rwandans were being butchered each day, U.S. officials shunned the term "genocide," for fear of being obliged to act. The United States in fact did virtually nothing "to try to limit what occurred." Indeed, staying out of Rwanda was an explicit U.S. policy objective.

With the grace of one grown practiced at public remorse, the President gripped the lectern with both hands and looked across the dais at the Rwandan officials and survivors who surrounded him. Making eye contact and shaking his head, he explained, "It may seem strange to you here, especially the many of you who lost members of your family, but all over the world there were people like me sitting in offices, day after day after day, who *did not fully appreciate* [pause] the depth [pause] and the speed [pause] with which you were being engulfed by this *unimaginable* terror."

Clinton chose his words with characteristic care. It was true that although top U.S. officials could not help knowing the basic facts—thousands of Rwandans were dying every day—that were being reported in the morning papers, many did not "fully appreciate" the meaning. In the first three weeks of the genocide, the most influential American policymakers portrayed (and, they insist, perceived) the deaths not as atrocities or the components and symptoms of genocide but as wartime "casualties"—the deaths of combatants or those caught between them in a civil war.

Yet this formulation avoids the critical issue of whether Clinton and his close advisers might reasonably have been expected to "fully appreciate" the true dimensions and nature of the massacres. During the first three days of the killings, U.S. diplomats in Rwanda

Photo on previous page: Secretary of State Warren Christopher's lack of interest in and knowledge of Africa posed key impediments to U.S. involvement in Rwanda. (**AP Images.**)

reported back to Washington that well-armed extremists were intent on eliminating the Tutsi. And the American press spoke of the door-to-door hunting of unarmed civilians. By the end of the second week, informed nongovernmental groups had already begun to call on the Administration to use the term "genocide," causing diplomats and lawyers at the State Department to begin debating the word's applicability soon thereafter. In order not to appreciate that genocide or something close to it was under way, U.S. officials had to ignore public reports and internal intelligence and debate.

The story of U.S. policy during the genocide in Rwanda is not a story of willful complicity with evil. U.S. officials did not sit around and conspire to allow genocide to happen. But whatever their convictions about "never again," many of them did sit around, and they most certainly did allow genocide to happen. In examining how and why the United States failed Rwanda, we see that without strong leadership, the system will incline toward risk-averse policy choices. We also see that with the possibility of deploying U.S. troops to Rwanda taken off the table early on—and with crises elsewhere in the world unfolding—the slaughter never received the top-level attention it deserved. Domestic political forces that might have pressed for action were absent. And most U.S. officials opposed to American involvement in Rwanda were firmly convinced that they were doing all they could—and, most important, all they *should*—in light of competing American interests and a highly circumscribed understanding of what was "possible" for the United States to do. . . .

Ignorance and Somalia Were Key

The two tracks of events in Rwanda—simultaneous war and genocide—confused policymakers who had scant prior understanding of the country. Atrocities are often carried out in places that are not commonly visited, where outside expertise is limited. When country-specific knowledge is lacking, foreign governments become all the more likely to employ faulty analogies and to "fight the last war." The analogy employed by many of those who confronted the outbreak of killing in Rwanda was a peacekeeping intervention that had gone horribly wrong in Somalia.

> Secretary of State Warren Christopher knew little about Africa. At one meeting with his top advisers . . . he pulled an atlas off his shelf to help him locate [Rwanda].

On October 3, 1993, ten months after President [George H.W.] Bush had sent U.S. troops to Somalia as part of what had seemed a low-risk humanitarian mission, U.S. Army Rangers and Delta special forces in Somalia attempted to seize several top advisers to the warlord Mohammed Farah Aideed. Aideed's faction had ambushed and killed two dozen Pakistani peacekeepers, and the United States was striking back. But in the firefight that ensued, the Somali militia killed eighteen Americans, wounded seventy-three, and captured one Black Hawk helicopter pilot. Somali television broadcast both a video interview with the trembling, disoriented pilot and a gory procession in which the corpse of a U.S. Ranger was dragged through a Mogadishu [capital of Somalia] street.

On receiving word of these events, President Clinton cut short a trip to California and convened an urgent crisis-management meeting at the White House. When an aide began recapping the situation, an angry President interrupted him. "Cut the bullshit," Clinton snapped. "Let's work this out." "Work it out" meant walk out. Republican Congressional pressure was intense. Clinton appeared on American television the next day, called off the manhunt for Aideed, temporarily reinforced the troop presence, and announced that all U.S. forces would be home within six months. The Pentagon leadership concluded that peacekeeping in Africa meant trouble and that neither the White House nor Congress would stand by it when the chips were down. . . .

U.S. Diplomacy Had Three Weaknesses

Each of the American [political] actors dealing with Rwanda brought particular institutional interests and biases to his or her handling of the crisis. Secretary of State Warren Christopher knew little about Africa. At one meeting with his top advisers, several weeks after the plane crash,[1] he pulled an atlas off his shelf to help him locate the country. Belgian Foreign Minister Willie Claes recalls trying to discuss Rwanda with his American counterpart and being told, "I have other responsibilities." Officials in the State Department's Africa Bureau were, of course, better informed. Prudence Bushnell, the deputy assistant secretary, was one of them. The daughter of a diplomat, Bushnell had joined the foreign service in 1981, at the age of thirty-five. With her agile mind and sharp tongue, she had earned the attention of George Moose when she served under him at the U.S. embassy in Senegal. When Moose was named the secretary of state for African affairs in 1993, he made Bushnell his deputy. Just two weeks before the plane crash, the State Department had dispatched Bushnell and a colleague to Rwanda in an effort to contain the escalating violence and to spur the stalled peace process.

Unfortunately, for all the concern of the Americans familiar with Rwanda, their diplomacy suffered from three weaknesses. First, ahead of the plane crash, diplomats had repeatedly threatened to pull out UN peacekeepers in retaliation for the parties' failure to implement Arusha [peace accords]. These threats were of course counterproductive, because the very Hutu who opposed power-sharing wanted nothing more than a UN withdrawal. One senior U.S. official remembers, "The first response to trouble is 'Let's yank the peacekeepers.' But that is like believing that when children are misbehaving, the proper response is 'Let's send the baby-sitter home.'"

Second, before and during the massacres, U.S. diplomacy revealed its natural bias toward states and toward negotiations. Because most official contact occurs between representatives of states, U.S. officials were predisposed to trust the assurances of Rwandan officials, several of whom were plotting genocide behind the scenes. Those in the U.S. government who knew Rwanda best viewed the escalating violence with a diplomatic prejudice that left them both institutionally oriented toward the Rwandan government and reluctant to do anything to disrupt the peace process. An examination of the cable traffic from the U.S. embassy in Kigali [the capital of Rwanda] to Washington between the signing of the Arusha agreement and the downing of the presidential plane reveals that setbacks were perceived as "dangers to the peace process" more than as "dangers to Rwandans." American criticisms were deliberately and steadfastly leveled at "both sides," though Hutu government and militia forces were usually responsible.

> 'We were naive policy optimists, I suppose.'

The U.S. ambassador in Kigali, David Rawson, proved especially vulnerable to such bias. Rawson had grown up in Burundi, where his father, an American missionary, had set up a Quaker hospital. He entered the foreign service in 1971. When, in 1993, at age fifty-two, he was given the embassy in Rwanda, his first, he could not have been more intimate with the region, the culture, or the peril. He spoke the local language—almost unprecedented for an ambassador in Central Africa. But Rawson found it difficult to imagine the Rwandans who surrounded the President as conspirators in genocide. He issued pro forma demarches over [President Juvénal] Habyarimana's obstruction of power-sharing, but the cable traffic shows that he accepted the President's assurances that he was doing all he could. The U.S. investment in the peace process gave rise to a wishful tendency to see peace "around the corner." Rawson remembers, "We were naive policy optimists, I suppose. The fact that negotiations can't work is almost not one of the options open to people who care about peace. We were looking for the hopeful signs, not the dark signs. In fact, we were looking away from the dark signs . . . One of the things I learned and should have already known is that once you launch a process, it takes on its own momentum. I had said, 'Let's try this, and then if it doesn't work, we can back away.' But bureaucracies don't allow that. Once the Washington side buys into a process, it gets pursued, almost blindly." Even after the Hutu government began exterminating Tutsi, U.S. diplomats focused most of their efforts on "re-establishing a cease-fire" and "getting Arusha back on track."

The third problematic feature of U.S. diplomacy before and during the genocide was a tendency toward blindness bred by familiarity: the few people in Washington who were paying attention to Rwanda before Habyarimana's plane was shot down were those who had been tracking Rwanda for some time and had thus come to expect a certain level of ethnic violence from the region. And because the U.S. government had done little when some 40,000 people had been killed in Hutu-Tutsi violence in Burundi in October of 1993, these officials also knew that Washington was prepared to tolerate substantial bloodshed. When the massacres began in April, some U.S. regional specialists initially suspected that Rwanda was undergoing "another flare-up" that would involve another "acceptable" (if tragic) round of ethnic murder.

Rawson had read up on genocide before his posting to Rwanda, surveying what had become a relatively extensive scholarly literature on its causes. But although he expected internecine killing, he did not anticipate the scale at which it occurred. "Nothing in Rwandan culture or history could have led a person to that forecast," he says. "Most of us thought that if a war broke out, it would be quick, that these poor people didn't have the resources, the means, to fight a sophisticated war. I couldn't have known that they would do each other in with the most economic means." George Moose agrees: "We were psychologically and imaginatively too limited."

Americans Could Not Save Even Their Staff

David Rawson was sitting with his wife in their residence watching a taped broadcast of *The MacNeil/Lehrer NewsHour* when he heard the back-to-back explosions that signaled the destruction of President Habyarimana's plane. As the American ambassador, he was concerned primarily for American citizens, who, he feared, could be killed or injured in any outbreak of fighting. The United States made the decision to withdraw its personnel and nationals [the following day] on April 7. Penned into his house, Rawson did not feel that his presence was of any use. Looking back, he says, "Did we have a moral responsibility to stay there? Would it have made a difference? I don't know, but the killings were taking place in broad daylight while we were there. I didn't feel that we were achieving much."

Still, about 300 Rwandans from the neighborhood had gathered at Rawson's residence seeking refuge, and when the Americans cleared out, the local people were left to their fates. Rawson recalls, "I told the people who were there that we were leaving and the flag was coming down, and they would have to make their own choice about what to do. . . . Nobody really asked us to take them with us." Rawson says he could not help even those who worked closest to him. His chief steward, who served dinner and washed dishes at the house, called the ambassador from his home and pleaded, "We're in terrible danger. Please come and get us." Rawson says, "I had to tell him, 'We can't move. We can't come.'" The steward and his wife were killed.

Assistant Secretary Moose was away from Washington, so Prudence Bushnell, the acting assistant secretary, was made the director of the task force that managed the Rwanda evacuation. Her focus, like Rawson's, was on the fate of U.S. citizens. "I felt very strongly that my first obligation was to the Americans," she recalls. "I was sorry about the Rwandans, of course, but my job was to get our folks out. . . . Then again, people didn't know that it was a genocide. What I was told was, 'Look, Pru, these people do this from time to time.' We thought we'd be right back."

At a State Department press conference on April 8, Bushnell made an appearance and spoke gravely about the mounting violence in Rwanda and the status of Americans there. After she left the podium, Michael McCurry, the department spokesman, took her place and criticized foreign governments for preventing the screening of the Steven Spielberg film *Schindler's List*. "This film movingly portrays . . . the twentieth century's most horrible catastrophe," he said. "And it shows that even in the midst of genocide, one individual can make a difference." No one made any connection between Bushnell's remarks and McCurry's. Neither journalists nor officials in the United States were focused on the Tutsi.

> The brute fact of the slaughter failed to influence U.S. policy except in a negative way.

On April 9 and 10, in five different convoys, Ambassador Rawson and 250 Americans were evacuated from Kigali and other points. "When we left, the cars were stopped and searched," Rawson says. "It would have been impossible to get Tutsi through." All told, thirty-five local employees of the embassy were killed in the genocide. . . .

The Killings Were Clearly Visible

Whatever the inevitable imperfections of U.S. intelligence early on, the reports from Rwanda were severe enough to distinguish Hutu killers from ordinary combatants in civil war. And they certainly warranted directing additional U.S. intelligence assets toward the region—to snap satellite photos of large gatherings of Rwandan civilians or of mass graves, to intercept military communications, or to infiltrate the country in person. Though there is no evidence that senior policymakers deployed such assets, routine intelligence continued to pour in. On April 26 an unattributed intelligence memo titled "Responsibility for Massacres in Rwanda" reported that the ringleaders of the genocide, Colonel Théoneste Bagosora and his crisis committee, were determined to liquidate their opposition and exterminate the Tutsi populace. A May 9 Defense Intelligence Agency [DIA] report stated plainly that the Rwandan violence was not spontaneous but was directed by the government, with lists of victims prepared well in advance. The DIA observed that an "organized parallel effort of *genocide* [was] being implemented by the army to destroy the leadership of the Tutsi community."

From April 8 onward, media coverage featured eyewitness accounts describing the widespread targeting of Tutsi and the corpses piling up on Kigali's streets. American reporters relayed stories of missionaries and embassy officials who had been unable to save their Rwandan friends and neighbors from death. On April 9 a front-page *Washington Post* story quoted reports that the Rwandan employees of the major international relief agencies had been executed "in front of horrified expatriate staffers." On April 10 a *New York Times* front-page article quoted the Red Cross claim that "tens of thousands" were dead, 8,000 in Kigali alone, and that corpses were "in the houses, in the streets, everywhere." The *Post* the same day led its front-page story with a description of "a pile of corpses six feet high" outside the main hospital. On April 14 the *New York Times* reported the shooting and hacking to death of nearly 1,200 men, women, and children in the church where they had sought refuge. On April 19 Human Rights Watch, which had excellent sources on the ground in Rwanda, estimated the number of dead at 100,000 and called for use of the term "genocide." The 100,000 figure (which proved to be a gross underestimate) was picked up immediately by the Western media, endorsed by the Red Cross, and featured on the front page of the *Washington Post*. On April 24 the *Post* reported how "the heads and limbs of victims were sorted and piled neatly, a bone-chilling order in the midst of chaos that harked back to the Holocaust." President Clinton certainly could have known that a genocide was under way, if he had wanted to know.

> Even . . . when bodies were shown choking the Kagera River on the nightly news, the brute fact of the slaughter failed to influence U.S. policy except in a negative way.

Even after the reality of genocide in Rwanda had become irrefutable, when bodies were shown choking the Kagera River on the nightly news, the brute fact of the slaughter failed to influence U.S. policy except in a negative way. American officials, for a variety of reasons, shunned the use of what became known as "the g-word." They felt that using it would have obliged the United States to act, under the terms of the 1948 Genocide Convention. They also believed, understandably, that it would harm U.S. credibility to name the crime and then do nothing to stop it. A discussion paper on Rwanda, prepared by an official in the Office of the Secretary of Defense and dated May 1, testifies to the nature of official thinking. Regarding issues that might be brought up at the next interagency working group, it stated,

1. Genocide Investigation: Language that calls for an international investigation of human rights abuses and possible violations of the genocide convention. *Be Careful. Legal at State was worried about this yesterday— Genocide finding could commit [the U.S. government] to actually "do something."* [Emphasis added.]

Note

1. On April 6, 1994, a plane carrying the presidents of Rwanda and Burundi was shot down in Rwanda. This incident set in motion the Rwandan genocide.

The UN Peacekeeping Force Proved Inadequate

Linda Melvern

The United Nations' decision about a Rwanda peacekeeping mission came just a few days after its mission in Somalia had failed. According to Linda Melvern, that experience in another part of Africa conclusively shaped the subsequent meager response to Rwandan needs. The tiny UN contingent, under-equipped as well as under-informed, entered Rwanda on a mission that was to prove truly impossible, Melvern explains. Melvern is a widely published investigative journalist, with a specialty in coverage of Rwanda, and the author of several nonfiction books.

There was criticism after the genocide that the commander of the United Nations peacekeeping mission for Rwanda, a Canadian soldier, Major-General Roméo Dallaire, was inadequately briefed. Some years later Dallaire said that, had he known about the

SOURCE. Linda Melvern, *Conspiracy to Murder: The Rwandan Genocide*. London, United Kingdom: Verso, 2004. Copyright © Linda Melvern 2004. Reproduced by permission.

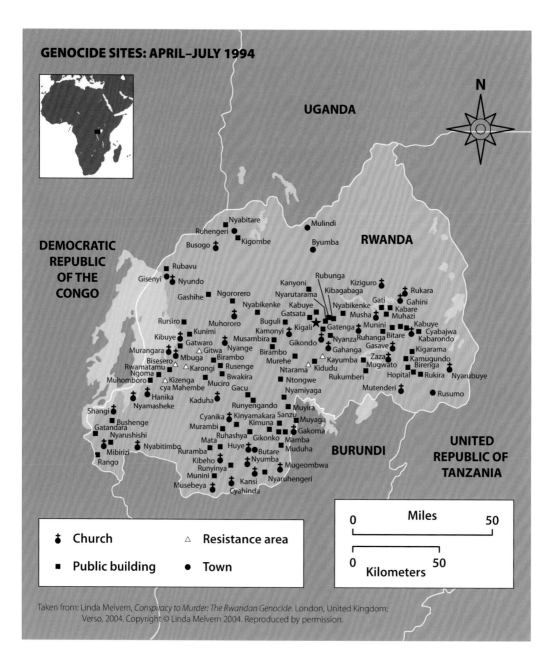

GENOCIDE SITES: APRIL–JULY 1994

Taken from: Linda Melvern, *Conspiracy to Murder: The Rwandan Genocide*. London, United Kingdom: Verso, 2004. Copyright © Linda Melvern 2004. Reproduced by permission.

human rights reports produced in 1993, he would have insisted on a much larger peacekeeping force from the start. Others said that nothing could have prepared him, or anyone else, for what was to come. Afterwards he speculated on this, his words suggesting the nature of a Greek tragedy: "You sort of wonder . . . when you look back at the whole thing . . . whether or not we were set up . . . whether or not the UN and myself fell into something that was beyond our ability to manage."

Major-General Dallaire was involved with the mission for Rwanda from the start. He had been appointed the chief of the UN Observer Mission Uganda-Rwanda (UNOMUR) established in May 1993 to strengthen a shaky ceasefire between the Rwandan army and the RPF [Rwandan Patriotic Front, a Tutsi-run force] and as one of 81 observers had been responsible for patrolling a buffer zone between them on the Rwanda and Uganda border. At the end of August 1993, Dallaire was asked to travel to UN headquarters in New York, where he was invited to head a reconnaissance mission for a proposed peacekeeping operation for Rwanda. No briefing documents had been prepared for him in New York and when he arrived in Rwanda, all he had was an encyclopaedic summary of Rwandan history, which his executive assistant, Major Brent Beardsley, had photocopied in a local library.

Dallaire's first visit to Kigali [the capital of Rwanda] came a few weeks after the Arusha Accords [peace agreements] were signed and everyone he met told him of their confidence in the peace agreement and of their belief that with the help of the UN the agreement could be implemented. There were some warnings about the dangers to come—the head of the gendarmerie, Major-General Augustin Ndindiliyimana, pointed out that there was no control over the distribution of weapons to civilians and he was told of the "hostile public information campaigns" aired by a privately owned radio station that was not supportive of the peace agreement—but by and large the mood was upbeat.

Consequently the initial report that Dallaire prepared about the peacekeeping mission achieving its goals was positive. He took part in the back-room deliberations to discuss it with officials at UN headquarters and diplomats recall his optimism. A determined soldier, Dallaire quite obviously enjoyed solving the problems that arise with a complex challenge; detail fascinated him and he developed a passionate commitment to the mission. Dallaire was an internationalist who had risen through the ranks and had waited his entire military career for a peacekeeping command.

> [Major-General Roméo] Dallaire had originally devised the operation for an estimated 8,000 troops.

On the face of it, the assignment was unambiguous. A three-year civil war had ended in peace, with a handshake between the government and invading rebels. There was to be reform of the corrupt regime and the creation of a power-sharing government. A timetable was agreed [to] that would lead to multi-party democracy. This was a classic, text-book peacekeeping mission.

France Pressed for Peacekeeping

It was France that had first suggested the idea of peacekeepers for Rwanda and her diplomats had aggressively lobbied members of the Security Council to agree to a mission. The French gave confidential assurances that the parties in Rwanda were truly committed to seeing the democratic process through to the end. There was not much enthusiasm from other permanent Council members, though. Two of them, the U.S. and the U.K., argued against help for Rwanda for reasons of economy. There were already seventeen UN operations and 80,000 peacekeepers worldwide and the U.S. was liable for a third of the peacekeeping bill. Congress was increasingly hostile towards the UN, and had been withholding its dues for years, almost bankrupting the organisation. The legislators in Washington were reluctant to appropriate any money at all, particularly for more UN peacekeeping, which was considered an abomination among some senior military in the Pentagon.

The Council itself was overwhelmed with problems in the UN missions in Cambodia, Somalia and the former Yugoslavia. Rwanda, in comparison, was quiet. There was not much time devoted to it.

The arguments in favour of UN help for Rwanda in the Security Council were persuasive, first from France and then most particularly from the Nigerian ambassador Ibrahim Gambari, who described Rwanda as a pathetic country, one of the poorest in the world. How could the west encourage this country to democratise, as the U.S. had done, and then turn its back? Gambari, one of the ten non-permanent members on the Council, said that there was a moral duty to help with the transition to democracy in Rwanda. There were complaints from the African group at the UN that resources were being monopolised in Europe to maintain the large and costly operation in the former Yugoslavia.

And yet each time the mission for Rwanda was discussed, there was insistence from the U.S. and the U.K. that any mission must be small and economical. This insistence had a decisive effect on the eventual mission. Dallaire had originally devised the operation for an estimated 8,000 troops. Reluctantly, he agreed that a responsible minimum was 4,500. This figure was pared down yet further by officials in the Secretariat even before it was put before the Council because the U.S. had hoped for no more than a symbolic presence of between 100 and 300 peacekeepers. Eventually a compromise total of 2,548 was agreed.

The report given to the Security Council by the UN Secretary-General Dr Boutros Boutros-Ghali on 24 September, 1993, requesting the creation of the mission for Rwanda, was optimistic. France, the one Council member with an intimate knowledge of Rwanda, had mounted a diplomatic campaign to convince its fellow members of the viability of the Arusha Accords. When the time came to discuss Rwanda, there was no mention of the human rights reports in the Council and nothing about a pattern of violence against the minority Tutsi. The author of the reports produced by the UN Commission on Human Rights, Bacre Waly Ndiaye, later said that had anyone asked his advice, he would have told the Council that the priority in Rwanda was the immediate protection of civilians at risk. The peacekeeping mission that the Council proposed for Rwanda was too small to make a difference.

> This evolution into high-cost, large-scale and open-ended missions found the [United Nations Security] Council soon overwhelmed in crises.

The Evolving Role of UN Peacekeeping Missions

For more than forty years, the UN peacekeepers had represented a pragmatic response to the Cold War. Peacekeeping, appropriately used, was an enormously useful device. It depended not on war-fighting soldiers but on troops trained in mediation and conciliation. A single peacekeeper at a check-point flying a UN flag was a symbol. The peacekeeper's weapon was not the rifle slung over the shoulder but his credibility; he represented a world community of states and the Security Council's will for peace. These UN troops were not expected to solve conflict but to monitor compliance with already agreed ceasefires; the operations were solely dependent on the co-operation of the relevant parties for their effectiveness. The range of operations throughout those first forty years—among them the UN Special Committee on the Balkans in 1946–1949 that monitored and investigated border violations between Greece and its neighbours; the UN Truce Supervision Organisation, sent to monitor the partition of Palestine in 1948; the

1956 UN Emergency Force, established to serve as a buffer between Egypt and Israel in Gaza and the Sinai Peninsula; and the 1960–1964 operation for the Congo, known by its French name, the Organisation des Nations Unies au Congo—was enormous.

With the end of the Cold War, a second phase of UN peacekeeping began. The UN force sent to Namibia to help its decolonisation from South Africa, for example, had a wider range of tasks than previous missions. The frequency of UN operations also grew steadily; between 1989 and 1994 there were eighteen new missions, more than had been dispatched in the UN's first forty-five years. This evolution into high-cost, large-scale and open-ended missions found the Council soon overwhelmed in crises. The blizzard of mandates, often ambiguous, inadequate and written with scant consideration of the realities on the ground, was impossible to respond to

The body of a U.S. soldier was dragged through the streets of Mogadishu, Somalia, on October 3, 1993. The UN Security Council vote on a peacekeeping mission in Rwanda came two days later and left Americans wary of the organization's efforts. (AFP/Getty Images.)

effectively; in Bosnia and Somalia, for instance, peace-keepers found they needed to rely on the use of limited but gradually intensifying armed force. And there were tragic mistakes, when the Council sent peacekeepers into situations with orders they could not follow, and which the council refused to change.

One of the ambassadors who was in the Council at that difficult time remembers: "We were a bunch of diplomatic amateurs." New Zealander Colin Keating said: "The UN . . . it's not ready to deal with all this." No one knew how to handle the new demands and complexities of the post Cold War world.

Disaster in Somalia

The UN's nemesis came in Mogadishu, Somalia, where the pitfalls of combining force with peacekeeping were finally and fully exposed. Somalia had been in a state of anarchy since 1992, with heavily armed gangs preventing the delivery of food aid and millions starving. Classified as the single worst humanitarian crisis in the world, President George Bush Snr. had sent thousands of U.S. troops there on a mission of humanitarianism as he was about to leave office in December 1992. President Bill Clinton had come to office in January 1993 committed to UN peacekeeping and promising to upgrade the size and professionalism of the UN headquarters staff, and he said he was willing for U.S. troops to come under UN command. In March 1993 the U.S. operation in Somalia was duly transferred to the UN and the mission immediately became more ambitious: its intention was to restore law and order and to compel the Somali militia to disarm. It was given all the powers of the Charter, Chapter VII, the enforcement powers. The U.S. ambassador to the UN, Madeleine Albright, was enthusiastic about the mission and she told the Council how in Somalia the UN was embarking on an unprecedented enterprise aimed at "nothing less than the restoration of an entire country."

But the operation went disastrously wrong. In June 1993, twenty-three Pakistani peacekeepers were hacked to pieces by rampaging mobs whilst trying to inspect weapons that were under UN supervision. Fifty more were seriously injured because of a lack of adequate equipment. After that, the Council mandated the UN troops, in Resolution 837, to arrest the warlord accused of having been responsible for inciting the crowds. The resolution emphasised the crucial importance of disarming the warlords and neutralising a radio station that was spreading anti-UN propaganda. From then on and throughout the summer months, an untold number of Somalis were killed as elite U.S. troops in raid after raid tried to find the warlord under suspicion for the Pakistani deaths. "It became a rogue operation," a UN lawyer said in New York. The high civilian casualty count was blamed partly on the Somali fighters' use of women and children as active participants, and at one point the U.S. shelled a hospital accusing the militia of using it as a vantage point. Although these U.S. operations were outside the command and control of the UN, it was the UN that was widely blamed and accused of flouting human rights with impunity. There were objections from other countries providing troops for Somalia; Italy threatened to pull out her 800 soldiers unless the U.S. stopped their "Rambo-like" raids. The Italian and Nigerian troops had almost come to blows at a roadblock about the interpretation of the mandate. The mission was a mess.

Worse was to come. On 3 October, 1993, in a hail of bullets and missile fire, elite U.S. troops who were attempting to arrest the warlord thought to be responsible for the Pakistani deaths ended up in a street battle with Somali fighters. A total of eighteen American servicemen lost their lives and eighty-four more were wounded. The U.S. troops had parachuted and driven into a residential area and had been pruned down by Somali fighters and trapped in a maze of tiny streets. In a terrifying night-time fire-fight, the U.S. troops had to be rescued by a UN peacekeeping force of soldiers from Malaya and Turkey driving Pakistani tanks. The battle in Mogadishu was the worst U.S. military humiliation since Vietnam, and the U.S. immediately announced, to the jubilation of the Somali warlords, that U.S. troops were pulling out of Somalia and urged all western nations to do the same.

The Reaction to Somalia

There remained the image, broadcast around the world, of the body of a U.S. serviceman dragged through the streets to a jeering and jubilant crowd. The Clinton administration distanced itself quickly and maintained correctly that the doomed mission had been "under the authority" of the UN, failing to mention that the attempt to arrest the warlord had been a U.S. operation. The Secretary-General, Boutros Boutros-Ghali, tried to distance the UN and blamed the U.S. The deaths had come in a failed U.S. operation, which had been convicted by U.S. troops without the UN either on the ground or in New York even being told, he said. Within days, the Clinton administration was accused in Congress of turning U.S. foreign policy over to feckless UN bureaucrats, and Boutros-Ghali was accused of Napoleon-like ambitions. A Peace Powers Act was immediately prepared to make it impossible for the president to commit any more troops to UN operations. The battle in Mogadishu had strengthened the hand of those in the U.S. Defense Department who had always wanted to distance the U.S. from UN missions.

The Security Council subsequently commissioned its own report on what had happened in Somalia and, after reading it, suppressed it. It outlined in graphic detail a

> The mission was intended to be small, it had the weakest possible mandate and it was to be run on a shoe-string.

UN mission completely out of control, with a patchwork command structure as unstable as it was dangerous and contingents refusing orders from UN commanders. One of the most serious weaknesses identified was a false assessment of the capability of the Somali fighters and the UN's lack of intelligence-gathering capability. The report recommended that the UN must return to peacekeeping, to the principles of consent, neutrality and impartiality. Impartiality was of paramount importance: peacekeeping only worked with a clear mandate and a will on the part of the people to achieve peace. The Council report recommended that never again should the UN undertake enforcement action. A peacekeeping official said: "The international community will be very careful in [the] future. We've learned that [troop contributing] states don't want to take casualties . . . you can't do coercive disarmament."

> 'Welcome to Rwanda, soldiers of the United Nations, soldiers of peace, soldiers of hope.'

It was two days after the deaths of the U.S. soldiers in the battle of Mogadishu that the Council was due to vote on whether or not to create a mission for Rwanda. So sudden and determined was the retreat from UN operations by the U.S. that many people thought that Rwanda would be lucky to get anything at all. In the end, the Council reached a compromise decision and on 5 October, 1993, the UN Assistance Mission for Rwanda (UNAMIR) was created under Resolution 872. The mission was intended to be small, it had the weakest possible mandate and it was to run on a shoestring. The persuading arguments had been that this was traditional peacekeeping and that the two most important ingredients were present—a ceasefire and a peace agreement. There was speculation that a deal was probably struck whereby French support in maintaining UN sanctions against Iraq helped to persuade a reluctant U.S. to vote for UNAMIR. However the vote came about, one thing was certain: from this moment on the Security Council would play a central role in the future of this tiny African country. . . .

The Ill-Equipped UN Force Arrived in Rwanda

It was plain to see just how half-hearted the United Nations effort for Rwanda really was. The force structure given to the peacekeepers, and in particular the equipment, bore no relationship to what was really needed. There were to be twenty-two armoured personnel carriers (APCs) and eight military helicopters to allow for a quick reaction ability. No helicopters arrived and only eight APCs were provided, of which five were serviceable. They did not arrive until March 1994 and they came direct from the UN mission in Mozambique without tools, spare parts or manuals. Most of the troops, some 942 soldiers, came from Bangladesh, but they had hardly any training. Dallaire tried to train them to create a quick reaction force but they were well below acceptable operational standard. Bangladesh was supposed to have provided a composite force of a medical company, an engineer squadron, a half-battalion of infantry and a movement control platoon.

The headquarters of UNAMIR was in a motel on the edge of eastern Kigali and on the road to the airport. It was a bleak and ugly concrete-block building whose tiny rooms each had a balcony looking over a desolate expanse of bare earth with a football stadium in the far distance. The stadium was to be used as transit accommodation for UN troops. Dallaire was followed by an advance team of twenty-one military personnel on 27 October. They spent their time sorting out a nightmare of logistics, steering a course through the bureaucratic UN labyrinth. They lacked everything, from telephones to desks and chairs. When the first troops arrived from Bangladesh, they had no bottled water or food; instructions issued by the Secretariat in New York that all contingents should be self-supporting had simply been ignored.

Although by 17 November, 1993, only a handful of peacekeepers had arrived, the headquarters was officially opened by President Juvénal Habyarimana, who, with his entourage, including members of his Presidential Guard, came to the hotel for a small ceremony. President Habyarimana expressed his gratitude for all the UN was doing: "Welcome to Rwanda, soldiers of the United Nations, soldiers of peace, soldiers of hope." The local press took lots of photographs.

But even while President Habyarimana and Dallaire exchanged pleasantries, that same night in northern Rwanda a series of grotesque massacres was taking place. There were five altogether, between the hours of 11 P.M. and 2 A.M. in the demilitarised zone north of Ruhengeri. A total of thirty-seven people, including women and children, were killed: the fathers and husbands were well known because they had just been successfully elected in their home communes. The spread of the killing, over a distance of more than 50 kilometres, gave the impression that they were carefully co-ordinated. In each case there was the same efficient elimination of witnesses, and no interest in stealing or destroying houses or furniture. Dallaire reported the news to UN headquarters in New York: "The swiftness, the callous efficiency and the ruthless number of men, women and children murdered principally by machetes and bayonets was obvious in this well orchestrated operation," he wrote.

There was another massacre at the end of November in Kabatwa in the north, near the Volcanoes National Park, when eighteen people were killed with knives and firearms. Again Dallaire reported back: "Examples of the atrocities include hands cut off, eyes pulled out, skulls crushed in, and pregnant women cut open." The day before, 29 November, six children and an adult had disappeared while collecting water in the national park.

They were later found tied and killed. Dallaire's military assistant, Brent Beardsley, was sent from the Kigali headquarters to investigate. After a long mountainous walk, he and his team found the bodies of the missing children. Each of them had been strangled by a rope and had a red burn mark round the neck. The girls had been gang raped. Some of the children had been hit on the head with a blunt instrument.

It was Beardsley's first week in Rwanda. He thought that it could not get any worse than this. . . .

The UN Mandate Did Not Change Even as the Situation Deteriorated

In early 1994 the hate radio station Radio-Télévision Libre des Mille Collines stepped up its broadcasts against the Arusha Accords, against opposition pro-democracy politicians, against the Tutsi and against the UN mission. The validity of the UN mission in Rwanda was increasingly challenged. It seemed at times as though peace never stood a chance. In order to try to explain the UN role in the country, Major-General Roméo Dallaire organised a press conference. No one came. Most of the local press was hostile to the UN, viewed peacekeepers with suspicion, and boycotted their briefings. The international press, at a time when exposing what was going on might have made a decisive difference, was simply not interested. What little international coverage there was on Rwanda described a tribal conflict between the "majority Hutu and minority Tutsi." Dallaire bemoaned the lack of international coverage not only of events but also of what the UN was trying to achieve in Rwanda. The grave problems that Rwanda faced were hardly a secret. Two of the most important aid agencies in Rwanda were clearly expecting a large number of casualties should the peace process collapse. The International Committee of the Red Cross (ICRC) and Médecins Sans Frontières [MSF] (France) began to stockpile medicines and water, and four huge tents were put up in the courtyard of the Centre Hospitalier de Kigali (CHK), the central hospital, to increase its capacity. The ICRC and MSF (Belgium) discussed how in the event of large numbers of casualties they would collect the wounded from the streets and which agency would provide emergency medical care. An expert logistician, Eric Bertin, who headed the MSF mission in Kigali, assessed the capacity of local clinics. In Geneva, the ICRC kept a medical team in reserve for Kigali. . . .

At the end of January, in one of his regular reports to Operational Command in Brussels, Colonel Marchal [of Belgium] said that this was now an impossible mission; the peacekeepers of UNAMIR had undertaken 924 mobile patrols, 320 foot patrols and established 306 control points. They had collected nine weapons. On 15 January, the Belgian ambassador in Kigali, Johan Swinnen, had written to his Foreign Ministry that the UN possessed proof of the existence of at least four secret arms dumps. He told the ministry that Dallaire had appealed to New York for new instructions concerning the mandate, and that UNAMIR must either be allowed to enforce the ban on arms in Kigali or be withdrawn. A way must be found, he told the ministry, to stop the continuing weapons distribution. . . .

Dallaire continued to try to get approval for more forceful action and tried to enlist the support of the UN Secretary-General's special representative, Jacques-Roger Booh-Booh. In a memo to Booh-Booh on 31 January, Dallaire warned, "The present security situation is deteriorating on a daily basis. Many groups seem to be directing their activities to violent attacks on ethnic and political opponents." A determined propaganda campaign was being waged against UNAMIR and the local media was "being used by a faction to incite ethnic, partisan and anti-UNAMIR activities." Dallaire pleaded for "determined and selective deterrent operations," which he argued were in accordance with peacekeeping doctrine, and the only way to gain the respect of the local population. In February, however, a cable from [UN Secretary-General] Kofi Annan reminded Dallaire that his mandate was modest and only authorised him "to contribute to the security of the city of Kigali . . . established by the parties": "We wish to stress that UNAMIR cannot, and probably does not have the capacity, to take over the maintenance of law and order in or outside Kigali. Public security and the maintenance of law and order is the responsibility of the authorities. It must remain their responsibility as is the case with all peacekeeping operations."

The Leader of the UN Peacekeeping Mission Explains Why It Failed

Roméo Dallaire

Sent in to Rwanda to lead a small United Nations peacekeeping unit before the genocide began, Canadian general Roméo Dallaire found himself in an impossible situation when the massacres started. As he explains in the following interview conducted for the PBS program *Frontline*, he did not have enough soldiers or equipment, and his UN supervisors advised him to avoid involvement and withdraw. Together with a general from Ghana, however, Dallaire stayed on and took action when he could. In the years after the genocide, Dallaire wrote a book about his Rwanda experience, testified before the international genocide tribunal, and became a member of the Canadian parliament. He struggled with depression in the wake of the massacres he witnessed but felt powerless to stop.

SOURCE. "Interview: with General Roméo Dallaire," *Frontline: Ghosts of Rwanda Interviews WGBH/Boston*, Fall 2003. Copyright © 1995–2010 WGBH Educational Foundation. Reproduced by permission.

Frontline: *What were your first impressions of Rwanda?*

Roméo Dallaire: What a phenomenal experience. You know the first breath of air of Africa—it felt like you were in another continent—you were, you were—and it was different. My skin, my senses felt that it was very significantly different, and as such you had to suck it in by the pores. . . .

It was incredible, just the adrenaline and the fact that what you were doing was going to provide the guidance for very senior people to decide whether or not these people would be helped or not in their path towards peace. I felt that as a very significant dimension of my responsibility. I mean, you were actually going to help them bring this about, because they couldn't do it on their own because of frictions and other reasons of that nature. And so the weight of that was real. The excitement of it was real. . . . [And I] felt a little nervousness, of course, first shaking hands with those leaders and starting up the mission. . . .

So on the day the [Rwandan] president's plane was shot down, April 6th [1994], where were you and what was the atmosphere then? Did you have a sense that something might happen?

On the evening of the 6th I was in my residence there with Brent Beardsley, my executive assistant, and the aide-de-camp (ADC) and a driver, and we were working on some administrative directives . . . At 8:30 the first phone call came in, saying that there had been a big explosion in Kinumbi camp, which is just at the end of the runway of the Kigali [capital of Rwanda] airfield, and saying that it looked like an ammunition dump that had exploded. . . . Soon after that the call came in and said, no, the presidential plane had crashed. . . .

And then there were phone calls from the prime minister, who confirmed that it was the presidential plane, and asking me for advice and what's going to happen now and the security situation. She wanted things to stay calm, in the capital particularly. And then a couple of other calls where she was saying she couldn't get in touch with many of her moderate cabinet colleagues, but more significantly all the hard-line members of the cabinet had disappeared, every one of them. They had all of a sudden vanished. While the moderate ones, she was getting various reports of them hiding or still there. But it was very difficult to get anybody together at that time.

What did you do then?

... The liaison officer called me and said that there was a crisis meeting being held at the army headquarters and they would very much want me to attend to assist. ... I took off with Brent Beardsley and my ADC and we went to army headquarters, and it was very quiet at that point and nothing much going on in the city. We attended the session with Colonel Bagosora, who was the executive assistant or chef de cabinet of the Minister of National Defense. He's a retired colonel and a hardline person, in fact considered even more than hardline. He was chairing the meeting. ... We had a number of exchanges explaining what I could do, what they wanted to do, dominated by the fact that I continued to insist that they should immediately get the Prime Minister Agathe [Uwilingiyimana] to come to the fore and be the political leader so that it'd be clear that this thing is not a military initiative one way or the other. And continuously Bagosora, acquiesced by the other senior officers there, kept saying that she is

> And as the day wore on it proved that there were a bunch of the troops that were absolutely useless and they were going to do absolutely nothing.

Roméo Dallaire (right), who headed the UN mission in Rwanda, said he "had no man-date" from the orga-nization to keep the peace. (Scott Peterson/ Getty Images.)

of no use and she never was able to garner her cabinet anyways. She was ineffective and not representative of the government, and that's why they, the military, were going to hold the fort for the shortest time possible and find the political structure that will come out of this and hand over to them.

Did you believe him?

Well at the time, I had no immediate feel that I was in the face of a coup d'etat. . . . However their not acknowledg-ing Agathe was that sort of signal to say, "Wait a minute, this is not necessarily as clear as it would seem. Bagosora was known to be a hardliner," and so on. Immediately you started to ponder, what was the aim of this exercise? . . .

I told [UN special representative for Rwanda Jacques Roger] Booh-Booh of my plan of action, which was to protect Agathe and get her to a radio station or some means of communicating with the population, so that she could express you know a calm to them. Because I was smelling more or more . . . that maybe this is not as clear as what we might think in regards to them simply trying to keep control of the situation. I was still not pondering coup d'etat as such, I was just [wondering] were they trying to maneuver and what did they consider to be the political process? And so I said, one thing for sure, we gotta keep Agathe protected. . . .

Immediately, There's a Stalemate

When you called [the UN headquarters in] New York, what was the message that you got back?

I was not an intervention force and that the rules of engagement were to be strictly self defense, and nothing more. There was a concern that we could get drawn into this exercise, and you can still see that paranoia of Somalia coming back, you know, "Just stay where you are, you are not in authority to intervene."

Now, in this UN stuff, the commander, although he has troops, they don't really belong to him. They're loaned by the country to the UN to be used, but each of these countries provide a contingent commander, a senior guy who communicates directly back to his capital. And so the contingents were over the course of the day getting more and more communications with their international capitals, who were becoming more and more restrictive in what they wanted their guys to do because the risk was too high, and the situation was too confused. And so we entered this arena where I had troops but I didn't have troops and how much of them could I use, and to what avail? And as the day wore on it proved that there were a bunch of the troops that were absolutely useless and they were going to do absolutely nothing. . . .

[I was also] trying to get the political meeting at nine o'clock at the American ambassador's residence sorted out, only to find out that the ambassadors couldn't make it there because there were more and more road blocks coming up and they were concerned about their security. . . . So the political process [was] going nowhere, and so we've got no data on what's happening. It made it only that much more significant that I had to go to where the source was . . . in order to get the sense of how much that side was going to try to stop this haemorrhage and go back to the Arusha agreement and to the rules of the weapons-secure area. . . .

> 'No way, I refuse to abandon the mission and turn tail and run while the bodies were piling up.'

We made our way to the Ministry of Defense [thinking that Bagosora might be there, but] nobody was there. I said, "Well, maybe they're right back to where they were last night in the army headquarters." . . . [So we] went to the main gate of the Kigali camp where the headquarters was, and that was armed to the teeth. . . . They were there with the armoured vehicles in a very strong defensive position. The major went out to see if Bagosora and the guys were there; in a very short time, he came back and said, "No, they're not there, they're at the École Supérieure Militaire (ASM) with all the commanders." So we just turned and went towards the ASM.

[Editor's note: While Dallaire was looking for Bagosora, the prime minister's house was stormed by Rwandan troops. The UN soldiers sent to protect her radioed back for instructions, and were told to adhere to the peacekeeping mandate, offer protection to the prime minister but not to use force. The prime minister fled to a neighbor's house, where she was later killed; the UN soldiers surrendered their weapons and were taken hostage by the Rwandans. The African UN soldiers were soon released, and the ten Belgian peacekeepers were taken away.]

At the secondary gate of the camp as we're driving by I saw two soldiers in the Belgian uniform lying on the ground about fifty odd meters inside, inside the camp, and I told the guy to stop. I said, "These are some of my guys." . . . I had already by then information that a number of my troops were unaccounted for, that I had Belgian soldiers already held up at the airport. I had a bunch of people that I didn't know what their state was in by the time I left. So that made me conscious of the fact that, "Hey, maybe they're not just held captive or something. I might be taking casualties." And that is the major shift in the whole operation at that point.

So by the time I'm objecting we're already at the ASM; it's only a hundred meters or so away; and at that point, the shock had turned into a rapid assessment of, "What the hell am I going to do now?" And in fact what it made me realize is that I had the bulk of my force, and also the civilians, in a very vulnerable position. I had over three hundred officers with no weapons or anything spread around the RGF [Rwanda Government Forces] side in particular for the security of the implementation of the peace agreement. . . .

Orders from the Top: Pull Out

Let me talk to you about the April UN Security Council maneuver and how it looked from your perspective. [UN Secretary-General Boutros] Boutros-Ghali had put forward the options for the withdraw—a cable came, and you were awakened at 4:30 [A.M.].

Yes. It's a cable that essentially is saying that there is no option for reinforcement, and that the options that are being studied are options of withdrawal or reduction of the force. It also indicates that although some countries—the British, the French—were inclined to [keep] a smaller force for a short period of time to see if there's any good will, the Americans come down categorically and say, "No, there's no way there's going to be a cease fire, so let's pull everybody out and get out of that quagmire and then see what happens afterwards."

. . . The Security Council was already of a mindset that for political reasons we should leave somebody on the ground, but they were certainly tending more and more to pulling out and following the lead of the Belgians and certainly the Americans. So it was a significant shift; forget any idea that somebody's going to come and help you Dallaire, or that your forces were going to actually do something positive. . . . So that scenario brought an enormous gloom. I remember Maurice Baril [military adviser to the secretary-general] sending me a code cable not long after, but because I was up north . . . Brent Beardsley took the phone call and Maurice said, "Tell Dallaire that there is no cavalry coming over the hill. None." . . .

As we got closer to the Security Council becoming far more involved with the process . . . Boutros-Ghali was being lobbied also extensively, and one of the options that came forward was that the whole outfit be pulled out. In fact I did get orders to pull out completely lock, stock and barrel from Boutros-Ghali and I said, "No way, I refuse to abandon the mission and turn tail and run while the bodies were piling up all over the goddamn place."

When I got that order, I went to [my deputy, the Ghanaian general Henry Anyidoho.] . . . I said, "Henry, they want us out. We've failed in the mission, we've failed in attempting to convince, we've failed the Rwandans. We are going to run and cut the losses, that's what they want us to do. What do you think about this?"

And Henry responded and he said—now remember he had a large force there, he had over eight hundred troops, and he took it upon himself without consulting, as yet, his government and he said, "We've not failed and we're not going to leave. We should stay." And that was all I needed because by Henry saying that, that meant that I would still have troops on the ground—which were good troops, not well equipped but good troops. . . . His support was exactly the depth that I needed to give me just that much more oomph to decide, yeah, that's it. So I stood up and I said, "Henry, we're staying, we're not going to run, we're not going to abandon the mission, and we will not be held in history as being accountable for the abandonment of the Rwandan people." It was just morally corrupt to do that. And that's when I went back and told them to go to hell, or words to that effect.

When the order came to start withdrawing down to the lowest level . . . to 270, well then I implemented a withdrawal plan. . . . We were able to stop the withdrawal of the Ghanaians and to keep about 450 on the ground. . . .

Were they operating beyond the mandate?

I had no mandate. UN had not given me it. I got orders on the 22nd of April, which is already over two weeks into the civil war and the genocide. But during that whole time there was no formal mandate. In fact they were trying to pull me out. And so we were operating by what we felt was right and what we could do, and it was under my instructions of what we can do that we used whatever forces that were willing to do things. . . .

These groups were responding to local demands, but then, pretty fast, within days of the start of this and the evacuation of the expatriates—all these white people, businessmen, abandoning the nannies who had raised their kids for years, with bags full of (certainly not) clothes, even bringing their dogs on the aircraft, [which is] against the rules. Running to the goddamn aircraft, running to the trucks to save their bums, and abandoning the ones who had been loyal to them for so many years . . . and a lot of them were Tutsis too. So we started to get these calls from New York . . . from here, there and everywhere, for us to go and save such and such. . . .

Certain Rwandans Were to Be Saved

You mean specific people.

Absolutely, yeah. . . . Now there was probably remorse while [those who had been evacuated from Rwanda] were sitting in Paris drinking their wine, so they got through channels to try and get us to save them, to pull them out. Other ones were very honest requests; like we saved a whole bunch of nuns from different religious orders. . . . Some of them were NGOs [nongovernmental organizations] that were very worried about their local staff because that's all they had on the ground. But a lot of them were also friends of people of influence and power who could put the squeeze on the UN, who could put the squeeze on me to go get them. So we were getting, both verbally and in writing, requests . . . to send guys to go find these people and try to save them. . . .

These guys were often unarmed, running through barriers, and then having to pick up these people and hide them in the vehicles to bring them through, because if the extremists found in any of our UN vehicles people like Tutsis and so on that we were protecting, then that was it. Every vehicle would be searched and all my people would be at risk. The risk was worth it to try to save people, but it became so abusive. I mean, Brent was managing at one time over 600 people on a list of special requests to help, and I got to the point that I told [them] in New York, "That's it. My people are being burned out and risking their lives, and sometimes nobody's there." It became a real difficult ethical problem for me. Why am I saving them more than anybody else, and why am I risking the lives of my observers and my staff to get them out more than anybody else? And so I entered into a debate about whether or not it was right.

We also had another dimension that all of a sudden came into this: the extremists had caught on to this, that we were at least going around and looking for people. And so what they would do was they'd go to places where they suspected had Tutsis or people hiding, and they would come in and tell people there, "This is the UN, we're here to save you," and all this kind of stuff. And people would climb out of the sewers or out of the ceilings and they'd slaughter them. That was the case, in fact, for the family of [Tutsi leader Paul] Kagame himself, who had put in a request for us to go [help them]. The guys went there, nobody was there. But they were seen going there. And so they came back and I said, "Well, try again the next day," because we did attempt that, too often. And when they came the next day, they were all slaughtered, all lying on the ground slaughtered in the house. So it started to get like, "Hey, are we helping people or are we guaranteeing them being slaughtered?"

Some Church Leaders Did What They Could to Help the Innocent

Marie Césarie Mukarwego

> In the following selection, Marie Césarie Mukarwego, a Catholic nun and an educator in Rwanda, explains that devotion to Christianity did not stop the killings in the majority-Catholic country. Fear paralyzed multitudes. The threat of death and the possibility of betrayal were pervasive. In this terrible situation, Mukarwego notes, some Catholic clergy found ways to diminish massacres and to enable people to leave Rwanda. Several years later, nuns led efforts toward reconciliation, which they recognized takes many years.

W hat one must understand is that the Church is made up of human beings and thus is not shielded from the fragility and weaknesses of our humanity. Those who massacred others during the

---

SOURCE. Marie Césarie Mukarwego, *Genocide in Rwanda: Complicity of the Churches?* St. Paul, MN: Paragon House, 2004. Copyright © 2004 by Paragon House. Reproduced by permission.

1994 genocide were for the most part Christians killing other Christians. The killers had heard the Gospel, many times, in fact. They were quite conscious of it. Some even spoke about it. Nevertheless, they chose to put the Gospel aside. They allowed themselves to be manipulated by those whose devilish project was the extermination of others.

Today [2004] in Rwanda, we are in the process of seeking reconciliation and justice through the *Gacaca* courts, where witnesses are asked to speak only about what they saw with their own eyes or heard with their own ears during the weeks and months of genocide in 1994. I shall try to do the same in this essay about the Church and the genocide in Rwanda, writing only about the experience I lived through, not about the rumors and stories I heard from others about that time.

> We broadcast a radio message which denounced violence, as well as ethnic and regional discrimination.

Before the Genocide of 1994: the Problem of Discrimination

One unfortunate fact is that in Rwanda there was discrimination against the Tutsis in the schools and public services. This discrimination was practiced by the Hutu-dominated government administrative authorities. For example, students could not freely enroll in schools, not even in Catholic schools, because enrollments were all centralized in the Ministry of Education, as they still are today. The Ministry decided who went where. We in the schools simply received lists of the pupils who were assigned to us.

What was the reaction of the Church to this practice? At one point, the Church asked the Ministry of Education if it could itself choose a certain percentage of student enrollment. We received permission to do so,

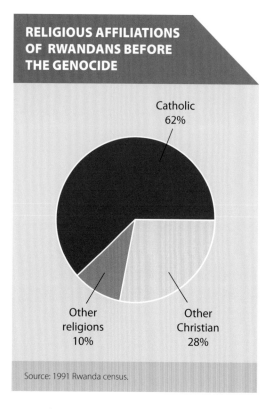

RELIGIOUS AFFILIATIONS OF RWANDANS BEFORE THE GENOCIDE

Catholic 62%

Other religions 10%

Other Christian 28%

Source: 1991 Rwanda census.

but then the Ministry required us to give back to them a list of our choices, which they would either approve or disapprove according to the Ministry's own criteria. In making our selection of pupils, we nuns, brothers and priests in our associations, decided to choose poor, less privileged, but intelligent children who were likely to be overlooked by the Ministry. With these percentages, however small, the Church wanted to correct the irregularities observed in the Ministry of the Education regarding how they selected pupils. Heads of schools also wanted the right to select pupils and ask for their admission to their schools. In this way, we thought certain corrections would be possible and that an active and real protest could be made about anomalies in the system.

I remember certain meetings I attended where the subject of free admissions to the schools was discussed frankly, but then quickly eclipsed by the authorities. We did succeed, however, in having one meeting, for a whole morning, with the President of Rwanda, Juvénal Habyarimana. We told him about certain problems we felt were debilitating the country. We said to him what we wanted to say, even though later we did not see much change. We also helped to organize other actions, more directly linked to the safety of people and public peace, such as the "Marches for Peace," organized from 1990 up to January 1994. These involved many Christians and their pastors.

Another activity I participated in concerned ASUMA, the Association of Major Superiors in Rwanda. The members of ASUMA visited all the country's prisons in 1990 after arrests were made of people suspected of being accessories of *Inkotanyi* (Rwandan Patriotic Army), the group which had launched an attack against Rwanda in 1990. With these visits, we tried to investigate the situation of the prisoners, tried to give them moral comfort and to submit a report supporting their release. We all knew these people were wrongfully held.

> No one among us imagined that the killers would go into the churches and into the houses where people had found refuge.

One year later, we organized visits to camps in Rwanda of displaced persons who had been unjustly deprived of their homes and were literally hostages of the parties in conflict. We took time as teams to listen to them, to be with them, and to work with them. Likewise, after the organization of an inter-African meeting of Major Superiors of Priests in Rwanda, we broadcast a radio message which denounced violence, as well as ethnic and regional discrimination. These examples, although modest, show us in support of the minorities and the innocent. . . .

Fear and Questions of Betrayal Grew

The Church, as an institution, has been put on trial for allegedly having prepared and carried out the genocide with the politicians with whom it was linked. This is both a shame and a scandal, for Rwandans and for foreigners. Did the Church betray its members, its sons and daughters?

What has been written about the Rwandan genocide by those who experienced its atrocities are expressions of their immense suffering and their wounds that are still bleeding. Revenge is the first reaction of those who have suffered so much, and the anger these atrocities provoked needs a scapegoat, one that can be heaped with violence and even with spite. The articles written by people who described the four months of the genocide said that priests had gathered people in the churches all over Rwanda in order to have them killed, and even that they had carried out the killings themselves.

People traditionally took refuge in the churches in times of trouble. Neither those who took refuge there, nor those who welcomed them, suspected what was going to happen. No one among us imagined that the killers would go into the churches and into the houses where people had found refuge. In general, the communities and pastors tried to do all that was in their power to save the people, but faced with a band of armed people, priests and brothers, whose hands were empty, who were without weapons or any means of defense, were powerless. We know that some non-violent priests and brothers were themselves killed along with those they tried to defend.

Refugees very quickly communicated their experiences as they traveled across the country. Their stories caused widespread fear. Many people, priests and nuns included, no longer dared to resist or even to welcome people into their churches and covenants because the threat of death was real. We were afraid to see people die. We were also afraid to die ourselves. This was not only true for the Christians. In the strongest sense of the term, all Rwandans were paralyzed and many no longer responded to pleas for help. In some places, even soldiers themselves were afraid of the militia and would not confront them.

In regard to the accusation that the Church—priests, brothers and nuns—handed people over, what in fact happened? The militia would arrive, demanding that everyone leave the confines of the house so the militia could check whether the occupants included any RPF [Rwandan Patriotic Front, a Tutsi-led group] accomplices. They also searched to see if there were any hidden weapons. Everyone was forced to leave the house. The *interahamwe* (Hutu militia) chose those they wanted

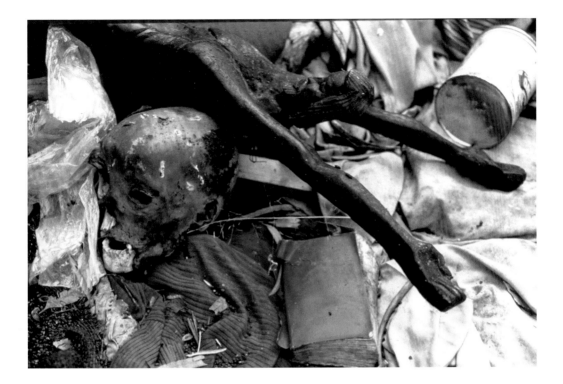

The skull of a slain Tutsi lies beneath a religious icon. Some Hutu members of the clergy were among the individuals who put themselves at risk to protect their fellow Rwandans from harm. (Scott Peterson/ Getty Images.)

and left the others. These scenes were repeated again and again. Today that is interpreted as a betrayal of the people who were being hidden, but few consider the psychological pressure that such a state of stress constitutes, or the fact that every day one was harassed and threatened with death.

Some Clergy and Church Leaders Tried to Prevent Killings

I ask myself: Is it really fair to say that the bishops said nothing during the genocide of 1994? It is true that the Church did not speak out. We did not have the courage to assume the consequences of speaking: insecurity, imprisonment, suffering, even death. But I remember speaking to a bishop on 16 April 1994, asking him to broadcast a message to the people to stop the slaughters, and to try to persuade the Christians involved to return to reason. He answered: "I have asked permission to broadcast a message by radio, but I was refused the opportunity to do it." Even if he had been able to obtain permission, it is doubtful whether he would have been able to speak freely.

In his book, Abbé Joseph Ngomanzungu draws attention to messages during the months of April to June 1994 that the bishops tried to make on the radio, without success, however. According to Abbé Ngomanzungu, Radio Rwanda refused to allow the broadcast of an official statement prepared by the bishops of Rwanda on 9 April 1994, in which they demanded that the authorities take care of the safety of the people and their goods, that they neutralize all those who were disturbing the peace, that soldiers protect everyone without distinction of ethnic group, party or area. Everything, they said, must be done to stop the bloodshed, and they urged Rwandan Christians to welcome those who were seeking refuge from the violence and killings. Other messages also were addressed to Rwandan authorities and to the Rwandan Patriotic Front (RPF) by various bishops and by the Episcopal Conference.

> Militia men in front were ready to fire on them. A single word saved them all.

To the foregoing, I can add the testimony of my Assumption communities. In one of them, Hutus and Tutsis were aligned against the wall to be killed. Militia men in front were ready to fire on them. A single word saved them all. A Sister recognized the head of the militia and called him by his name, saying, "You, so-and-so, you want to kill us?" He turned towards his men and shouted at them to leave the place. That is how these people were saved at the last minute. This man, head of the militia that came to that convent, is no longer alive.

In the same community, the Sisters and people who were taking refuge with them decided not to show their identity cards so as to confound the militia. It was a gesture of solidarity between the Sisters and the refugees, and among the whole group of refugees. Another group invented a ruse because they wanted to leave the country. They decided to hide their identity cards with their ethnic identity indicated and ask for certificates stating that they had lost their IDs, but still not saying what their ethnic group was. It was difficult to do, but they succeeded in leaving the country. In another community, a Hutu Sister hid Tutsi Sisters inside the convent and spent her day outside negotiating with the *interahamwe* so that they would not enter the house. She gave the militia men all the money that the community had in order to save the Sisters. They all survived; no one was killed. . . .

Bravery After the Genocide

Because there was so much killing, there needs to be as much repentance and a determination to live the message of Christ. In such a way, we can see in action the words of Jesus, "The truth will set you free." All those who have had the courage to face the truth are internally free, healed of their wounds, or they are in the process of being healed. This process of reconciliation has been experienced by all sorts of people— by Christians of modest means, by laity engaged in the Church, by civil servants, by priests, brothers and nuns. All affirm that they have been liberated as a result of confronting the truth about themselves and the events of 1994.

> We experienced moments of strong emotion, forgiveness and reconciliation.

A personal example is that of my own congregation. In 2000, the year of the Jubilee of the Catholic Church, the Sisters of the Assumption of Rwanda decided to record their history, beginning with their foundation in 1954 through the recent events of 1994 and to the year of jubilee. We did this within the framework of the *Gacaca-*

synods. During the Church's jubilee year, all our communities were encouraged to take the step of forgiveness as a congregation, purifying our memory "of all the failures, the regrettable errors and sins which have left their traces among us." Each province lived moments of reconciliation and forgiveness in the action of grace. Our province of Rwanda-Chad joined this movement by integrating the recent history of our country. The Sisters in communities told their stories and exposed their wounds. They discussed this history and sometimes questioned the people implicated in their lives. In this step, both personally and as a community, we experienced moments of strong emotion, forgiveness and reconciliation. As a result, we were able to celebrate together the joy of a resurrection for the province.

The process is ongoing because reconciliation is a life-long task. We are happy to carry the wounds of others and to combine the joy and the suffering of "the other" in absolute transparency and with great confidence.

We live together, Hutus and Tutsis. Our daily struggle is to accept our differences—differences of opinion about the recent history of our country, and other differences too. If there is interpersonal conflict, we agreed we would examine it, trying to reconcile ourselves without allowing resentment or bitterness to become reestablished among us.

People are getting accustomed to speaking "the truth" to one another, and they are becoming freer to ask questions which might even embarrass the authorities. They have learned how to assume responsibility for their lives and actions. It is necessary that we continue on this path without tiring.

Catholic Church Leaders Made Matters Worse

Tom Ndahiro

In the following viewpoint, Tom Ndahiro asserts that, for years, leaders of the Catholic Church in Rwanda helped spread and deepen a racist ideology that was used to justify the genocide. Then, he alleges, after the killings, church leaders were either silent about their responsibility or unrepentant. Some leaders' comments were parallel to Nazi statements, Ndahiro avers. Missing throughout, he notes, was a public commitment to the Christian role of unity under God. Tom Ndahiro, a journalist, has served as a member of the Rwandan National Human Rights Commission.

All over Rwandan hills, valleys and mountains, thousands of crosses mark the mass graves of victims of the 1994 genocide. During the genocide, many Tutsis were massacred in or around places of worship, including Catholic churches—paradoxically, in

SOURCE. Tom Ndahiro, *Genocide in Rwanda: Complicity of the Churches?* St. Paul, MN: Paragon House, 2004. Copyright © 2004 by Paragon House. Reproduced by permission.

a country which was the most Christianised in Africa, with Christians constituting more than eighty percent of the population. Catholic bishops in Rwanda have sometimes claimed that all Rwandans believe in God. There are hundreds of churches and chapels everywhere and almost every day the faithful repeatedly recite the prayer, "Our Father who art in heaven," pleading with God, the Father, to deliver them from evil (Matthew 6:13). From where, then, did the malevolence at the root of the genocide come? How and by whom could it have been overcome? Part of the answer to these questions lies with the Church and its members.

In the book of the prophet Isaiah, we read, ". . . reject evil and do what is good" (Isaiah 7:15), an admonition that can bring authentic deliverance. It is an unfortunate fact that most of those involved in organising the whole process leading to the genocide were people who were baptised Christians. Some were in the Church hierarchy, particularly in the Roman Catholic Church, which is the focus of this paper. By omission and/or commission, some members of the Catholic Church's leadership were involved in the 1994 genocide against Tutsis. Considering what genocide is—by definition, or as a crime—the involvement of an institution like the Catholic Church demands painstaking analysis.

> In Rwanda, the leadership of the Christian Churches, especially that of the Catholic Church, played a central role in the creation and furtherance of racist ideology.

The Church Had a Role in the Creation of Exterminationist Ideology

According to Jean-Pierre Karegeye, a Jesuit priest, genocide is morally hideous, an evil expressed by forgetting God, and hence a new form of atheism. Karegeye asks several pertinent questions which merit consideration: "Christians killing other Christians? How could

Rwandan Christians who manifested commitment to their faith have acted with such intense cruelty? How did ordinary people come to commit extraordinary evil . . . ? Does the sin of genocide disturb the relationship between God and the perpetrators in official Catholic Church discourse? How can we explain the strange situation of priests involved in the crimes of genocide who are still running parishes in Western countries? Why are they protected by the Vatican against any legal proceedings?" He concludes: "The Church's attitude towards genocide seems to suggest that the hierarchy of religious values is not usually in proportion to the hierarchy of moral standards."

Generally, in Rwanda, the leadership of the Christian Churches, especially that of the Catholic Church, played a central role in the creation and furtherance of racist ideology. They fostered a system which Europeans introduced and they encouraged. The building blocks of this ideology were numerous, but one can mention a few—first, the racist vision of Rwandan society that the missionaries and colonialists imposed by developing the thesis about which groups came first and last to populate the country (these are the Hamitic and Bantu myths); second, by rigidly controlling historical and anthropological research; third, by reconfiguring Rwandan society through the manipulation of ethnic identities (from their vague socio-political nature in the pre-colonial period, these identities gradually became racial). From the late 1950s, some concepts became distorted; thus, democracy became numerical or demographic democracy. The philosophy of *rubanda nyamwinshi*, a Kinyarwanda expression which politically came to mean "the Hutu majority," prevailed after the so-called social revolution of 1959 and ignored the basic tenets of democracy. In my view, recurrent genocides in Rwanda since 1959 were meant to maintain the "majority" by killing "the other." Distributive justice became equivalent to regional and

Rwanda's genocide had roots in racist ideologies intertwined with Christianity as it was introduced alongside colonialism. (**AP Images.**)

ethnic quotas, and revolution came to mean the legitimised genocide of the Tutsis.

Church authorities contributed to the spread of racist theories mainly through the schools and seminaries over which they exercised control. The elite who ruled the country after independence from Belgium in 1962 trained in these schools. . . .

Church Authorities Did Not Repent

It is difficult to describe the position taken by the institutional Church just before and during the genocide. It is appropriate to take note of a declaration made by some "Christians" who met in London in 1996: "The church is sick. The historical roots of this sickness lie in part with the 'mother churches.' She is facing the most serious crisis in her history. The church has failed in her mission, and lost her credibility, particularly since the genocide. She needs to repent before God and Rwandan society, and seek healing from God."

> Since October 1990, the Church had employed the official language of hate propagated by the government.

This diagnosis offers a good summary of the situation. The Church lacks a sense of remorse and therefore cannot repent; hence, its active involvement, in my view, is the last stage of genocide—denial. At the time when the Church's voice was needed most, its authorities abided by the Commandment to maintain Hutu "unity" in order to fight the common "enemy." Since October 1990, the Church had employed the official language of hate propagated by the government. The minor difference was in the medium of communication. While the government used national radio and other print media, the Catholic Church made use of Pastoral Letters.

The writings of the Catholic bishops just after 1 October 1990 read like an official text from the state publishing house. After the attack by the RPF [the Tutsi-led Rwandan Patriotic Front], President [Juvénal] Habyarimana continually referred to them as "aggressors" or "assailants." The official media followed suit. The French fortnightly *La Relève* commented, "During the morning of October 1st, 1990, Rwanda was attacked by assailants including Rwandan refugees, members of the Ugandan army who rallied with Ugandan elements, members of this army."

In the Catholic bishops' letter of 7 November 1990 entitled "Happy are the artisans of peace, for they will be called Sons of God," the same words were used, with some emphasis to confirm that the President had spoken nothing but the truth in his speech on 5 October 1990. But that was not the only similarity. The President had also said: "Aggression against our country is not only of military nature. It also rests on international media manipulation and disinformation . . . we were surprised by the violent manipulations, being prepared a long time ago, as we now know, by certain media from the West and not of the least minimal. Our country is still being subjected to attacks and calumnies, to systematic lies, that we can only qualify as diabolic in nature." And in their letter, the bishops said: "In these difficult times, it is our duty to remain in solidarity in the defense of the truth. . . . False information and rumors, libel and lies have been spread in Rwanda. . . . We strongly deplore disinformation, cleverly and maliciously organized by those who have attacked Rwanda, about certain facts and events which some of the media have transmitted."

Remaining in solidarity with the government that planned genocide was not limited to speeches in the name of defending "the truth." The "*comité de contacts,*" bringing Catholics and Protestants together, was created as a messenger of the government. This ecumenical movement is hailed in several documents as proof that "the Church did something" during the genocide. Father Joseph Ngomanzungu recently dedicated almost a whole book to this committee. His publication exhibits the failures and complicity of an institution he is trying to defend.

On 2 March 1993, a delegation of the "*comité de contacts*" met the RPF at the Papal envoy's residence in Bujumbura, Burundi. The aim was for the representative

Church leaders to discuss with the RPF ways and means of bringing the collapsed peace process back on track. Deliberations centered on the circumstances that had led the RPF to attack the government forces on 8 February that year, and what could be done to reverse the trend. This twelve-hour meeting followed another that had brought together the RPF and the four opposition parties. In the latter, it had been agreed that: "Despite the content of the cease-fire accord concluded between the Rwandese Government and RPF on 12 July 1992, the blood of innocent persons continues to be shed in all regions of Bugesera, Ruhengeri, Gisenyi and Kibuye. This organised terrorism, which has totally paralysed the government, has been transformed into a real genocide which has shocked and revolted the universal consciousness and which constitutes a serious violation of the cease-fire accord."

> 'A [Tutsi] is deeply bad, not because of her education, but because of her nature.'

Despite explanations and requests to the bishops at least to condemn what was happening, there was no positive response. With the exception of Bishop Alexis Birindabagabo of the Anglican Church, who proposed that there had to be a statement to condemn the killings that were by then common knowledge, others remained indifferent. It is disquieting to read that in that meeting, Bishop Augustin Misago of the Diocese of Gikongoro said that the death of Tutsis was not enough reason to justify the usurpation of power. Misago's comments in fact give the impression of a racist without scruple, who attached no value to the life of Tutsis. He remained committed to the Hutus rather than to God's commandment. During the genocide, he refused to hide any Tutsis, for "lack of space" in his bishop's residence. Except for Bishop Birindabagabo, this *"comité de contacts,"* whose president was Bishop Thaddée Nsengiyumva of Kabgayi, remained loyal to the regime that committed genocide. Their statements, available today in the publications of Father Joseph Ngomanzungu, are a testament to the team's sympathy with the perpetrators of genocide—before, during and after the genocide.

A Bishop Condemns Tutsi Women in Particular

Like Archbishop [André] Perraudin, Bishop Focas Nikwigize of Ruhengeri was unequivocal in supporting the ideology of genocide. While in exile in Goma, Zaire, he told a Belgian newspaper,

> The Batutsi [Tutsi] would like to restore their power and to reduce the Bahutu [Hutu] to slaves! Their objective was to take Kigali [the capital of Rwanda] by force, whatever the cost; not to share power, but to govern. In order to fulfill this objective they used two sorts of weapons: their guns, which came from Europe, and their women. They gave their women to Europeans and so remained in a strong alliance with them. That is how bad they are! A Muhutu [Hutu] is simple and right but a Mututsi [Tutsi] is cunning and hypocritical. They seem fine, polite and charming, but when the time comes, they force themselves on you. A Mututsi is deeply bad, not because of her education, but because of her nature.

The above statement bears witness to the racist views of this priest. Considering a people as naturally bad is similar to the explanation used by the Nazis to justify the extermination of Jews in order to maintain the purity of the Aryan race. Bishop Nikwigize continues: "What happened in 1994 was something very human. When someone attacks you, you have to defend yourself. In such a situation, you forget that you are a Christian; you are first a human being."

There has been no condemnation of Bishop Nikwigize's denial and endorsement of the genocide from the Church hierarchy as a whole, nor has there been an admonition from any individual bishop. Since "silence implies consent," one might rightly say that the Church leaders who have said nothing have espoused Nikwigize's ideas. It was all the more disquieting that the justification of the genocide came from a senior Church leader whose influence was great among refugees. . . .

The Aim Should Be Unity

I chose to write about the Catholic Church and the genocide in Rwanda because I would argue that it was the only institution involved in all the stages of genocide. As a layperson, it is astounding to hear about the "love, truth and trust" that the Church has achieved in a country where genocide took more than 800,000 lives in just a hundred days, and to see the institutional Church protecting, instead of punishing or at least denouncing, those among its leadership or in its membership who are accused of genocide.

There is no doubt that throughout the history of Rwanda, Church leaders have had ties with the political powers in Rwanda. The Church was also involved in the policy of ethnic division which degenerated into ethnic hatred. In order to succeed in its mission of uniting people, the Church in Rwanda and elsewhere must examine its attitudes, practices and policies that have too often encouraged ethnic division. If all Christians belong to the same family of God whose head is Jesus Christ, the message that must prevail in the Church, to paraphrase the Apostle Paul, is that there is no Hutu, Twa and Tutsi—but simply Rwandans. The Church should embody and emulate what St. Paul says: "There is neither Jew nor Greek, there is neither slave nor free, there is neither male nor female; for all you are one in Christ" (Galatians 3:28).

Women Were Active Participants in the Slaughter

Derek Summerfield

In the following selection, Derek Summerfield maintains that female leaders in the Rwandan national and local governments, teachers, nurses, and nuns joined men in carrying out the massacres. Other women participated in different ways: cheering on the killers, stripping the dying of their possessions, and betraying their neighbors, friends, and even relatives. Deeper analysis is necessary, Summerfield asserts, to determine why this happened—why women of all walks of life participated so avidly. Derek Summerfield, who grew up in South Africa, is a British psychiatrist and author with a deep interest in human rights.

SOURCE. Derek Summerfield, "Rwanda: When Women Become Killers," *Lancet*, vol. 347, June 29, 1996, pp. 1816–1817. Copyright © 1996 Elsevier Limited. All rights reserved. With permission of Elsevier.

What happens to the minds of ordinary, law-abiding citizens when those in authority urge them to identify neighbours and colleagues as the "enemy"? We need only look to Germany in the 1930s, Bosnia, and Rwanda. One facet of this resonant question concerns women. Accounts of war generally assign women the role of victim, but an important publication by African Rights, a London-based human rights organisation, documents how in Rwanda in 1994 women were active participants in genocide.

The 100 days of killing in Rwanda was not a spontaneous outburst but was instigated and driven by those holding political, military, and administrative posts. Civil servants, journalists, businessmen, judges, academics, priests, teachers, students, doctors, nurses, traders, and staff of local and international agencies were involved, directly or indirectly. Many of these were women, with

Women from various levels of Rwandan society—like these Hutu refugees, shown while interned for their alleged complicity—took part in the killing. (Malcolm Linton/ Getty Images.)

the educated providing encouragement and role models for the illiterate. Two women ministers in the interim government promoted genocide, one of whom was Pauline Nyiramasuhuko, the Minister for Women and the Family. She visited refugee camps and supervised the slaughter of hundreds of Tutsi men.

Educated women from every walk of life participated actively. Some of the most cruel local government officials organising the killings, especially in Kigali [the capital of Rwanda], were women. African Rights concludes that teachers played a key role, but also documents how nuns closed the door on their desperate parishioners, or handed people over to the militias. Sister Julienne Kizito, from the convent at the Monastery of Sovu, Butare, spent three months in the company of local killers. Eyewitnesses recall how she handed out petrol and then watched as people were burnt alive. Such nuns and priests were, no doubt, encouraged by the stance of senior churchmen (including archbishops) of both the Roman Catholic and Anglican churches, who had close connections with the Hutu government, failed to protest against the murders, and issued intentionally misleading statements.

> At Kibuye Hospital, a nurse marked Tutsi children [for killing] by shaving their heads.

Even Medical Staffs Participated

About a hundred nuns and priests were murdered, including Hutus who refused to embrace the extremists' cause. Hostels, health centres, and maternity clinics were turned into slaughterhouses, Tutsi medical staff being prime targets because of their education and status. Patients and staff were macheted or blown apart by grenades thrown into clinics. The largest massacre at the University Hostel of Butare was on April 28, 1994, [and] was facilitated by doctors and nurses who identified their

Tutsi colleagues and patients and betrayed their hiding places. At Kibuye Hospital, a nurse marked Tutsi children by shaving their heads.

Elsewhere, women joined machete-wielding mobs that surrounded places of refuge. Some acted as cheerleaders, ululating the killers into action, and stripped the dead and barely living of their jewellery, money, and clothes. They betrayed their own neighbours, friends, and relatives to the militia. Just as some men refused to host people their wives had agreed to protect, some women hounded out fugitives hidden by their husbands.

Responsibility for the genocide started with its chief male architects, whose strategy was to involve as much of the population as possible. How this worked, particularly how ordinary Hutu women were mobilised, needs the closest possible analysis, both in respect of specifically Rwandan factors and those that might be more generally applicable.

Many of the prominent perpetrators of genocide are in exile, including several nuns who are being sheltered by their religious order in Belgium. A number of well-attested killers, including ex-Minister Pauline Nyiranasuhuko, have found their way onto the payroll of international aid agencies serving victims. And the proposed war crimes tribunals face huge logistic difficulties.

Accusing Children of Participating in the Genocide Raised Legal and Moral Issues

Judith Matloff

In the following selection, Judith Matloff explains that, more than two years after the Rwandan genocide, more than two thousand children remained in jail on charges of participating. But Rwandan laws and international precedents appeared inadequate to assess their possible punishment, and the judicial system was overwhelmed in general. Meanwhile, she states, conditions in most of the prisons were terrible, and imprisoned adults abused the boys. Matloff, who teaches at the Columbia University Graduate School of Journalism, was a foreign correspondent for 20 years in areas such as Rwanda, Sudan, Chechnya, and Moscow.

SOURCE. Judith Matloff, "Rwanda's Bind: Trying Children for Genocide," *Christian Science Monitor*, vol. 89, January 28, 1997. Copyright © 1997 The Christian Science Publishing Society. All rights reserved. Reproduced by permission from *Christian Science Monitor* (www.csmonitor.com).

Years after Rwanda's genocide ended, thousands of minors remained incarcerated for their alleged involvement in the event. (Alexander Joe/AFP/Getty Images.)

Claude is like most other eight-year-old boys. He likes a good game of soccer and a cuddle from his mother. But the boy is not a typical youngster. He is accused of taking part in Rwanda's genocide, murdering his neighbors by throwing a grenade into their house.

Claude is one of 2,137 minors held in Rwandan detention centers [as of January 1997] as genocide suspects. In 1994, up to 1 million Tutsis and moderate Hutus were killed in ethnic fighting.

For up to 2½ years, Claude and the others have languished in detention centers without being formally charged—under conditions appalling even for adults— posing a complicated moral issue for children's rights activists watching from the sidelines.

"This is the first time in contemporary history, certainly since the Second World War, that we have children accused of crimes against humanity," says Ray Torres of UNICEF's children's protection unit in Rwanda.

"Children have certainly been involved in such crimes in Nicaragua, Cambodia, Sierra Leone, and Liberia. But they were never arrested or accused of it. And certainly not in such staggering numbers."

> Without a doubt, many children were encouraged to follow the example of the adults who led the terror.

The crux of the moral problem is that Rwandan law, while providing leniency for minors, does not provide for punishment of juvenile crimes of such magnitude. And there are few precedents from elsewhere in the world to guide decisions.

And, as Save the Children officials point out, the implication of minors in such crimes challenges the traditional interpretation of childhood and youngsters' capacity to break the law.

Jailed Children Are Sexually Abused

The United Nations Convention on the Rights of the Child, adopted in 1989, defines childhood as below the age of 18. But in Rwanda, children as young as 7 are entrusted with adult responsibilities such as tending cattle and younger siblings.

The crimes include acting as informants for the Hutu militias that orchestrated the genocide, arson, rape, theft, and murder. Without a doubt, many children were encouraged to follow the example of the adults who led the terror.

But while groups such as UNICEF do not advocate impunity for the children who took part, they question how to teach right from wrong without ruining a young life. They argue that keeping children in jails where it is widely recognized that they are sexually abused by adults may not be the right answer.

The situation was deemed so grave by UNICEF that it took the unprecedented step of building prisons and special wings for minors to separate them from the adults. "This is the first time UNICEF was confronted with something like this," Mr. Torres explains. "Normally, we advocate deinstitutionalization for such children. But we felt we had to do something in this case because there was a life-threatening situation."

The boys receive little sympathy from Rwanda's largely Tutsi authorities, who are overwhelmed by an inadequate judicial system that has only 16 trained lawyers and no juvenile experts. Authorities argue that they have enough trouble coping with prisons overcrowded with some 90,000 genocide suspects. They say they cannot make special allowances for children, some of whose ages are difficult to verify for lack of records.

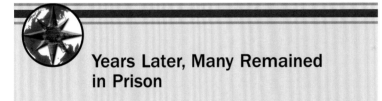

Years Later, Many Remained in Prison

In 2009, fifteen years after the genocide, about 70,000 Rwandans were in prison on charges of genocide-related crimes. Up to 30,000 more were released that year, according to Reuters, mostly those who had confessed to lesser roles.

Those released included sick and elderly people and those imprisoned when they were younger than 18. They still faced possible charges in traditional village courts.

A decade after the massacre, up to 24,000 prisoners were released, most of them also children, elderly and ill people, and those who had been imprisoned for as long as allowed under the penalties they faced.

In addition, some Rwandan authorities harbor hatred of the Hutu majority, which carried out the genocide, and have little sympathy for those sitting in festering jails. "The conditions may not be the best. But we do not have any resources," says Francois Mugernanganga, director of Gitarama prison where 42 minors are housed among the 6,688 adult prisoners.

> Experts . . . say the children may be safer in jail in some cases than outside.

Gitarama is deemed one of the "better" prisons because it is less overcrowded. But the overpowering stench of urine and feces and years of unwashed bodies assaults the nose. Thousands of shirtless men sit on the filthy floor because there is nothing else to do. Their meager belongings—thin blankets and cardboard boxes donated by the Red Cross—hang on the wall because there is no other space.

There is a separate quarter for minors. But it has no door, and even warders admit that grown men can sneak in at night to rape and abuse the boys.

Questions of Innocence and Privilege Arise

Two boys, who say they are 16, protested their innocence, saying that envious neighbors denounced them as murderers to steal their cattle and property.

"I was at home when the murders took place," insists a boy named Barundi.

"I don't even know the names of the people who I supposedly killed," says the other, named Sebahire.

Before he can give more details, the nervous guards abruptly end the interview, which has lasted only five minutes. "That's enough," one says, marching the boys back to the courtyard that serves as a giant cell.

Back at Gitagata, young Claude is among the fortunate 197 who stay at the reformatory detention center 25 miles south of the capital, Kigali. Inmates were under 14 at the time of their alleged crime and thus deemed not criminally responsible. Some are as young as 8 now.

A further 109 boys who were also under 14 at the time of the genocide should have also been transferred to Gitagata, but are still detained in prisons or jails. Authorities cannot say when their transfer will take place.

At Gitagata, the children live better than some free Rwandans, eating regular meals of porridge, beans, and peas. They attend classes with children from the nearby villages. They play sports. In fact, word got out in the prisons that life was so much better in Gitagata that some teenagers lied about their age to get in. (They were found out and transferred back to prison.)

Where Can a Child Be Safe?

But there is a downside, which director Louis de Montfort finds so demoralizing that he thinks of resigning from his job. The boys sleep four to a bunk bed, with rats scurrying in the dormitory. Bigger children pick on the littler ones. The boys live with constant uncertainty of when they will be freed. Their parents often are too scared of reprisals to visit them.

Worse, Mr. De Montfort suspects that many of the boys may be innocent.

Like the adults interviewed in the prisons, nearly all the minors insist on their innocence. The closest any one of the dozens interviewed came to admitting guilt was a depressed 11-year-old in an oversized red sweater that came down to his knees.

Asked why he was at Gitagata, he replied simply, "War is bad."

In theory, the first trials of minors are to begin in March [1997]. But with the judicial overload, many say the beleaguered judicial system cannot cope.

Impunity is out of the question. And experts like De Montfort say the children may be safer in jail in some cases than outside. He cites a Save the Children report released last year that surveyed views of survivors of the genocide.

Many surveyed say the fact that children participated in the genocide meant that they could not be considered children anymore. In others words, the children could face severe ostracization and possible attacks if they were released from prison.

"Reintegration is a 50-50 thing," De Montfort says. "Fifty percent, the child has to be ready. Fifty percent, the community has to be ready. The problem is, when do we really know if the child is safe?"

[Editor's note: Starting in 2001, the younger half of the jailed children were freed after reeducation. Many of the rest were imprisoned until late 2009.]

Another Genocide Could Happen Anytime

Jonathan Curiel

The conditions that preceded the slaughter in Rwanda appear in other countries, according to Jonathan Curiel, and the reluctance of great powers to intervene also persists. So it is unrealistic to simply say genocide will never again happen, even when there are ample warnings and indicators of its likelihood. In regard to Africa, Curiel asserts, race is clearly a factor. Isolation from Western attention is another. Self-delusion needs to be avoided, he maintains—the nations of the world must realistically assess the situation and be ready to act decisively to prevent genocide. A San Franciso–based journalist, Curiel is the author of *Al' America: Travels Through America's Arab and Islamic Roots.*

SOURCE. Jonathan Curiel, "The Future of Genocide Is Unfortunately Very Bright," *San Francisco Chronicle*, April 11, 2004, p. E1. Copyright © 2004 Hearst Communications Inc., Hearst Newspaper Division. Reproduced by permission.

While the numbers change, the vows stay the same. After 11 million people (including 6 million Jews) were exterminated in World War II, the world said, "Never again." After 1.7 million people were confirmed dead from Pol Pot's murderous rule in Cambodia, the world said, "Never again." After the tragedy of Rwanda, when 800,000 people were massacred in three months, the world said, "Never again."

Can it happen again? It's hard to believe it cannot. Genocide always makes a comeback somewhere in the world.

Wednesday [April 7, 2004] marked the 10-year anniversary of Rwanda's genocide. In a pilgrimage of respect, representatives from every hemisphere flew to Rwanda's capital, Kigali, to express their sorrow and to witness the country's attempts to move on. Kofi Annan has already apologized for the United Nations' failure to stop Rwanda's murders. So has former President Bill Clinton, who has said he'll "always regret" not taking more action against the Hutu extremists who used machetes, clubs and other crude weapons to kill their victims.

Unfortunately, there may always be more genocides for which to apologize. Even today, alarming atrocities occur out of the glare of international attention.

For example, in Sudan. Because of fighting in the western part of the country, almost 1 million ethnic Sudanese have been forced to flee their villages in the past year, while thousands of their countrymen reportedly have been murdered and raped by government-backed militias. The perpetrators are of Arab descent (Sudan is a member of the Arab League); the victims are non-Arab tribespeople. Nine days ago, Human Rights Watch issued a scathing report about the brutality, but it generated little outrage or media attention.

> Beyond the issues of race and will are the practical impediments to stopping genocide.

For example, in Ethiopia. In the past five months, hundreds of Anuak—an indigenous people living near the country's western border with Sudan—have been killed, apparently with the tacit support of the government in Addis Ababa, which is trying to resettle other Ethiopians onto the land.

What Are African Lives Worth?

"The world knows nothing about this," says Gregory Stanton, a former State Department official who heads Genocide Watch, based in Washington. "There are only 100,000 Anuak left on the face of the Earth, and the Ethiopian government has declared that it wants to resettle about a million highland Ethiopians into the lowland areas where the Anuak live. So, ethnically cleansing them and moving them off and getting them to move to Sudan is government policy."

Stanton calls it genocide. He also has a theory (also voiced by others, including Rwandans) about why Western governments are reluctant to get involved when genocide happens in Africa: That atrocities against blacks there don't count as much as atrocities against Americans or Europeans that happen anywhere in the world. Ten years ago, there was no international political will to stop the Rwandan genocide.

"We still have not come to the point where African lives are worth as much as (other) lives in the eyes of many people," Stanton says. "I think it's racism. It's too bad that we're still in that era, that we don't see that we're all part of the human race."

Beyond the issues of race and will are the practical impediments to stopping genocide. The United Nations doesn't have an armed force it can easily dispatch. It doesn't have an effective monitoring system for genocide.

These shortcomings exist despite the fact that U.N. member countries supposedly adhere to a convention—

Despite remedies that followed the Rwandan genocide, similar events—destruction at the hands of the janjaweed militia in Sudan's Darfur region, for example—have not been forestalled. (Scott Nelson/Getty Images.)

adopted in 1948, after the horrors of the Holocaust—that requires them to prevent genocide anywhere it happens. (When Rwanda's murders began on April 7, 1994, the United States sent Marines to rescue American citizens in Rwanda, but for the next month, Washington officials refused to utter the word "genocide" to describe the killings there—despite knowing that atrocities were being committed. By April 21, 1994, Hutu extremists had already killed 100,000 people.)

Annan admitted the U.N.'s shortcomings at a major genocide conference three months ago in Stockholm. There he announced his support for a special envoy on the prevention of genocide, a new U.N. position that would report directly to the Security Council. Ten years ago, when the U.N.'s top commander in Rwanda, Gen. Romeo Dallaire, cabled his bosses in New York to warn of an impending slaughter, his pleas fell into a bureaucratic black hole. They were discounted by top brass, including

Annan (who was then in charge of U.N. peacekeeping). Dragged down by the U.N.'s indifference, Dallaire was powerless to stop the widespread killings, which quickly escalated and lasted for 100 brutal days.

Genocide Potential Simmered for Decades

Waves of killings of Tutsis, as far back as the 1950s, preceded the 1994 slaughter. Rwanda should have been on some kind of genocide watch list, but it wasn't.

Alison Des Forges, a Rwanda expert who is senior adviser to the African division of Human Rights Watch, says the international community ignored warning signs in Rwanda, including the government's categorization of citizens along ethnic lines. In a policy that stemmed from Belgium's former colonial rule, Rwandans were forced to carry identity cards that listed themselves as Tutsi or Hutu.

> Experts say genocide almost always happens in countries run by despots, military figures or other unelected leaders.

In the early 1990s, an extremist Hutu radio station in Rwanda (Radio RTLM) repeatedly broadcast messages of hate against Tutsis. A pro-Hutu newspaper (*Kangura*) also published tracts in the 1990s encouraging ethnic hatred against Tutsis, including a "commandment" that warned, "Tutsi are blood and power thirsty. They want to impose their hegemony on the Rwandan people by cannon and sword." All of this was on public record before April 7, 1994, when Hutu extremists reacted to the death of Rwandan President Juvénal Habyarimana by unleashing their fury.

"Full-blown genocide grows out of decades of ethnic tension, racial hatred, that builds up and reaches a climax when it mutates into full-blown genocide," says William Schabas, a Rwanda expert who is professor of law and director of the Irish Centre for Human Rights at National

University of Ireland in Galway. "Prior to that, you have waves of ethnic cleansing and other forms of persecution of a vulnerable minority. And that continues to go on in the world."

Experts say genocide almost always happens in countries run by despots, military figures or other unelected leaders. As in Sudan today, these countries often ignore human-rights pleas from outside the country, so it becomes a question of international resolve: How much is the Security Council or the United States willing to do to stop potential bloodshed?

Not much, it appears, in some cases. In her Human Rights Watch report titled, "Rwanda: Lessons Learned," Des Forges writes that Washington considered jamming the messages of hate on Radio RTLM in 1994, but considered it too expensive. The cost: $8,000 an hour.

Some Are Becoming More Realistic

The world is easily distracted from far-away atrocities. In mid-June 1994, when the full extent of Rwanda's killings were first being made public, the stabbing death of O.J. Simpson's wife dominated news coverage in the United States. The troubles of an ex-football star trumped the deaths of almost 1 million Africans.

"When I founded Genocide Watch," Stanton says, "my aim was, 'We won't let genocide happen again. If you guys aren't going to do anything about it, we're going to vote you out of office,'" he says. Pausing a bit to reflect on the likelihood that genocide will be stopped, he says, "It's going to be a long battle."

At the genocide conference in Stockholm, Annan suggested genocide will be a lasting problem. In his keynote speech he said, "I long for the day when we can say with confidence that, confronted with a new Rwanda . . . the world would respond effectively, and in good time. But let us not delude ourselves."

Annan's observation may be a healthy development.

"It's a more hopeful sign than you might think, because it indicates a realistic appreciation of the situation of the world," says Des Forges. "If you have that, then you can be prepared to do something. If you go around with blinders on saying, 'Never again, never again, never again,' then you're not prepared to act."

CHAPTER 3

Personal Narratives

Struggling as the Only Surgeon in Kigali

John Sundin

The Rwandan capital city of Kigali's only surgeon during much of the worst of the genocide was John Sundin, a 44-year-old American. During his weeks of incredible stress, Sundin faxed letters to a friend in New Haven, Connecticut, where he had worked. His letters describe the seemingly endless stream of patients Sundin and other medical personnel treated at a make-shift Red Cross hospital. In addition to coping with insufficient medical supplies and facilities, Sundin and the others dealt with threats issued by armed Hutu militias. John Sundin left his job as a Yale University School of Medicine instructor in 1994 to volunteer for the Red Cross in Rwanda. The previous year he served in embattled Sri Lanka.

Photo on previous page: A member of a Hutu militia displays his badge and the sheath for his blade. (**Scott Peterson/ Getty Images.**)

May 13

I'm living and working at a Red Cross field hospital that was set up a month ago in a converted Catholic convent. It is situated on a hill, looking out over the green hills of Rwanda. Rwanda is known as the Switzerland of Africa, but the comparison stops at the landscape. The country is ravaged by a savage war between the government—Hutu—and the "rebels"—Tutsi. Two tribes, two politics—very complicated. It's war, nevertheless, fought not with planes, bombs, tanks, or missiles but rather with rifles and mortars, and with a fair share of less sophisticated weapons: machetes, clubs, and spears.

Today started at a leisurely pace. There are seven people on the medical team, and we have about two hundred patients staying on the floor and in tents. I am the surgeon, and work with two nurses in our two operating rooms, which were classrooms a month ago. Our

The stress of performing surgeries during the Rwandan genocide had the complicating factor of regular threats to the lives of medical personnel there. (Guenter Schiffmann/Getty Images.)

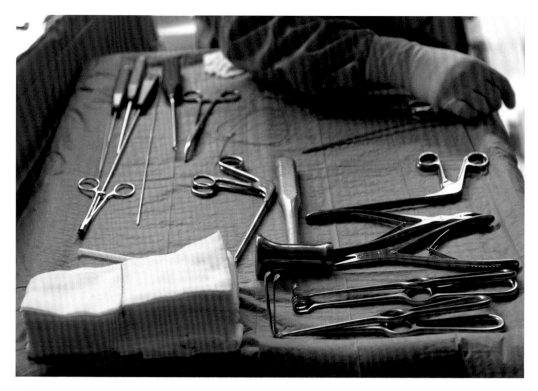

cases today included the closure of the scalp over the machete-exposed temporal lobe of a boy. Another: finishing touches on a leg blown off last week by a mine. A woman who, four days ago, was nine months pregnant—until someone clubbed her badly and she delivered a dead baby too quickly. She needed her vagina sewn up. A leg that I thought would have to be amputated looked okay, so I will look again in a few days. And this was a good day! I've done maybe twenty amputations of legs, hands, and an eye over the last week.

> Must rest. Must get better. Must choose. Crazy place.

Sometimes the taste of flesh and pus stay on my palate after the day's work. It's hard to sit down and eat meat, but I do because at night the international team—French, Swiss, Dutch, Danish, Finnish, and me (the American)—sits around a table. We eat what we have, and drink what we can, and smoke like there's no tomorrow. Then to sleep to the sounds of gunfire and awake to start again.

May 15

I'm dragging. To the operating room. Cover a machete cut to the skull four inches long with exposed brain. Nasty. He will probably die. After lunch I return to my room—sleep is what I need. Three weeks here seem like a year. I check my temperature; I have a fever of 101. That's a good sign—it's not stress alone that's making me feel so bad but some tangible pathogen. Water and aspirin and vitamin C. Fever now 102. Fitful sleep, this side of delirium. Stretchers, thousands of stretchers. Like Chaplin's *Modern Times*—an assembly line of stretchers and wounds, wounds, wounds. There's no other doctor here, so I'll have to treat myself. Dangerous. What's wrong with me? The flu? Dengue fever? Encephalitis? Malaria? Nothing is worse than to be sick far from home.

My friends nurse me. Aspirin, Fanta, soup. Doctors are the worst patients.

Night falls and my fever rises. Yes, it could be malaria. Kigali is a thousand meters high, but there are still mosquitoes and malaria. We have two drugs here that can treat malaria: Fansidar and Lariam. Neither is to be taken willy-nilly. A complication of Fansidar is called Stevens-Johnson syndrome, also known as Watch-every-square-inch-of-your-skin-drop-off syndrome. I saw a photo of it in a medical text. The odds? 1 in 10,000, 1 in 100,000. The odds of being eaten by a lion in New Haven are astronomically low, but if you are the one eaten by an escaped Barnum & Bailey lion then those reassuring odds are only statistics. Lariam—my own stock from Yale—can cause acute psychosis. I'll sleep on it. If my temperature is still up in the morning then I'll do something.

Sleep. Sweet sleep. Sweaty sleep. Mosquito nightmares. The sun again. The thermometer again. Higher, not lower: 103 and pushing 104. Brain-frying time. My head aches to the hair roots. Must treat myself. Fansidar or Lariam? Skin loss or psychosis? What a choice. Convoluted synapses. Feverish thinking. I decide on the Fansidar—all I have to lose is my skin. Better my skin than my mind.

Now the nurse from hell arrives. She's Dutch. Maybe fifty something, and looks like she was sired from stick insects. She's good—don't get me wrong. A veteran of Mogadishu, Kabul, etc. However, I suspect sometimes that she thinks we are in Amsterdam, not Kigali. Limits have to be set.

Anyway, this nurse knocks on my door, enters, and sits on my bed. I know there's trouble brewing. A new patient, twenty something, with a shrapnel wound in his left flank. Blood in his urine. Trouble. The left flank is where the kidney and the big aorta live. I'm dizzy even thinking about getting vertical, but there's no other surgeon. I operate and he may die anyway. I don't operate and he dies for sure. I operate and I am sick for three more days. I don't operate and rest, and can operate in a few days. Too late for him in a few days. Others may come in tomorrow. Must rest. Must get better. Must choose. Crazy place. No lawyers, only limits.

She pushes as she always does: "Well, he will die if we don't operate." I know she's right, but "No, I won't operate today" rolls off my tongue.

Charges: breach of Hippocratic oath. Plea: temporarily crazy place. Sentence: loss of all skin.

May 16

Recovered from my fever and my Fansidar dose with my skin gill intact. The flank wound died as expected. The team was eating together at the time of the news, and we all discussed our limits. The insect nurse is pushing to do more and more and more. Get blood donors! Fight to save every double amputee! It's her nature. The rest of the nurses (French, Swiss, Danish, Finnish) are more willing to accept the limits: very little backup, a sea of wounded, and limited supplies, including blood. Sure we could do a liver resection if we had to, but with no blood, oxygen, or ventilators, the patient is as good as dead anyway. I sense she faults me for not having operated yesterday—but sometimes, *c'est la vie, c'est la mort.*

May 21

Yesterday a man came in with his personality on the stretcher after getting shrapnel to the head. We have a zombie now. A woman buried alive in a mass grave dug herself out after twelve hours. She's pretty freaked out. I would be.

May 25

Bunkered in today. Mortar hit Red Cross compound next door, killing two and wounding five. Hospital staff leaves and wounded pour in. Fifty more today. Putting them everywhere on the Found now. No more tents. Sixty out of one hundred staff have left. Twenty cases to operate on but tomorrow will be another day of shelling. Phillip, our four-pack-a-day Swiss director, reassured us today that we were not a political target, only in a bad geographic place. Politically correct, geographically incorrect.

May 27

The situation is evolving—now very, very tense. Today, for the first time, I feared for my life. Shelling all day, bunkered in. Patients lying on stretchers for three days, waiting for surgery and dying. Patients are dropped off at the gate screaming. Before the military hospital was closed down, we were getting 90 percent Tutsi patients, and the Hutus went to the military hospital. Now everyone comes to us. We are becoming the nexus for these warring, century-old tribal hatreds.

> I hid in a corner today, fully expecting to be murdered.

Extremists still exist. The Hutu militia showed up at the hospital today with Kalashnikovs and clubs with spikes. These are the folks who kill Tutsi for sport—and they're in the hospital! They want to know why we treat Tutsi before Hutu. We can't even tell who is Tutsi and who is Hutu. They want to know what happened to one of their men who was brought in yesterday. He's dead. He was a fat man with a small hole up over his liver. There were five others ahead of him with their bellies sliced open. Twenty others with mangled limbs. Now they accuse us of killing this man. They want his body. They take our walkie-talkies. The local staff is in a panic. These are crazed armed killers, the same bunch who killed 150 patients in a Médecins Sans Frontières hospital in Butare. Two staff leave through the back door saying, "It's finished, it's finished." I am finally really scared. We all are.

The militia take two Red Cross workers, Andre and Ischelle, to find the body, which is already buried in our own mass grave in the compound. They see the body has no surgery marks. They want his shoes. They say he had a million Rwandese francs in them. Not there now. They have murder in their eyes.

The U.N. arrives, only by coincidence. They want some bandages. The militia leaves with the body. They say they will be back. Foreboding. We have no security anymore. Our local staff has left. The military can't be trusted. They're about to be overrun.

I hid in a corner today, fully expecting to be murdered. They wanted the medical team that's "not treating their people." That's me: I'm the surgeon, the only one. This is really no joke. The locals see it, too. "They don't play games," a local says about the militia. The mortars have been a nuisance—a low probability of being hit—but now we are marked by killers who live down the road.

At Yale, we used to have weekly morbidity and mortality meetings where the surgeons tore one another apart like pit bulls for as little as a wound infection. Tame compared with the jury in this crazy place.

We are no longer safe, and the medical team knows it. Mortars are one thing, but killers are another. Tomorrow at sunrise we will give our decision: We cannot spend another day in the hospital with Kalashs at our heads. We get U.N. protection or we request evacuation as a group. We just can't do any more. Sacrificing our lives isn't in the job description. The chaos is peaking. Order is dissolving.

I'm too tired to be dramatic, but believe me, the situation is very, very, very tense. Please don't tell my mother.

June 11

It's happening: I'm burning out. I really noticed it yesterday while amputating a rotten leg at the mid-thigh, my back and hands sore, my gag reflex twitching. We had fifteen cases between 9 and 1—arms and legs to cut off or dress, a nose and two eyes blown away, a five-year-old leg connected by a thread of flesh. In the beginning we had a schedule. I saw wounds healing and grafts taking. I used to know the patients. Now there are so many wounded that it's assembly-line first aid.

There's another man on the ward with a very bad leg. He refused amputation a few days ago. He missed his chance. He's got the "gas" now—gas gangrene up to his flank. He'll rot from the leg up, like the others. He'll start to smell and the flies will come to feast and the nurses will say do something and I'll say no. I'll send him to our "hospice" tent and then I'll put him out of his misery.

I've lost my sense of humor. I'm beginning to feel a certain distance. People are beginning to look like insects. Bad sign. The end is not in sight on the military or political front. The end is not in sight for the wounded. But my end is in sight. I'm going to leave at the end of June. Three weeks seem like a very long time. Will I make it? Suddenly the edge has lost its romance.

A Prominent Woman Escapes Death

Monique Mujawamariya, interviewed by Armande Saint-Jean

In the following interview with Armande Saint-Jean for *Ms.* magazine, a leader of the Rwandan Human Rights League describes, just months after the genocide, how she barely escaped being killed. She describes the roots of the conflict—a repression by a dictator and his militia—as well as the special struggles of Rwandan women, and what should and will happen next. She says the United Nations could have easily prevented the massacre but now pays a greater cost. After escaping Rwanda, Monique Mujawamariya moved to Montreal, Canada, where she founded and was president of Mobilisation Enfants du Monde.

SOURCE. Armande Saint-Jean, "Rwanda: An Activist Reflects on Her Nation's Trauma and Recovery with Monique Mujawamariya," *Ms.*, vol. 5, November 1994, pp. 10–15. Copyright © 1994 Lang Communications. Reproduced by permission of *Ms.* magazine and the author.

*M*s. interviewed Rwandan human rights activist Monique Mujawamariya in August [1994] in Montreal, where she had taken refuge with her children. Trained as a social worker, Mujawamariya, 39, has served as executive secretary of the Rwandan Human Rights League for the past four years—a position that placed her in immediate danger when the president of Rwanda, Juvénal Habyarimana, was killed in a mysterious plane crash on April 6, 1994.

Shortly thereafter, members of the Hutu-dominated government launched a campaign of genocide against the minority Tutsi, who, at the time, made up close to 15 percent of Rwanda's 7.5 million people. It is now estimated that more than 500,000 unarmed Rwandans, mostly Tutsis, were massacred. Hutu government officials and civilians who had advocated power-sharing with the Tutsis as part of a more democratic government were also murdered. In addition, approximately 75,000 Rwandans have died from disease and starvation in refugee camps in Burundi, Tanzania, and Zaire. Most of the refugees are Hutus who feared retaliation by the Tutsi-led Rwandan Patriotic Front (RPF), which forced out the Hutu government in July, when most of the fighting stopped. Human rights observers say that the RPF is responsible for killing some Hutu civilians, although on a much smaller scale. But tens of thousands of Rwandans remain displaced and much of the country is in ruins. . . .

> I spent a week in the rafters of my house.

[Upon] Rwanda's independence in 1962, Hutus took control of the government; they remained in power until July of this year. The government of Rwanda has been responsible for discrimination and violence against the Tutsis for more than three decades. Sporadic massacres have forced upward of a half million Tutsis to flee the country. Civil war broke out in 1990, when the

RPF, which was organized by exiled Tutsis in Uganda, invaded Rwanda. Opposition parties were legalized in July 1991, and a cease-fire was established in 1992. Peace accords were signed in August 1993, which obligated Habyarimana's authoritarian regime to form a coalition government with opposition parties, including the RPF.

But even before the 1993 accords, a growing civilian opposition movement, involving moderate Hutus as well as Tutsis, had forced Habyarimana to begin democratic reforms. (Many opposition members believe that Habyarimana was assassinated by those in his own party opposed to any power-sharing with Tutsis.) Human rights activists like Mujawamariya, who is Hutu, risked their lives to bring international attention to human rights abuses in Rwanda, where Tutsi women were routinely raped by soldiers, and tens of thousands of Tutsi civilians were jailed or killed for being "accomplices" of the RPF. Activists in Rwanda and abroad also accused the RPF of some human rights abuses.

As Mujawamariya explains below, when the timetable for democratic reform accelerated, so did the attempts of Hutu hard-liners in the government to retain power: arms were distributed by the army to the "youth wings" of government-affiliated parties; state-controlled radio stations stepped up their propaganda, inciting attacks by identifying scores of Tutsis and moderate Hutus as "traitors." Mujawamariya herself bears facial scars from a suspicious car accident, which she believes was engineered by the government.

She Felt Pressure All Around

Mujawamariya was interviewed for *Ms.* by Armande Saint-Jean, a journalist and professor of communications at the Université de Sherbrooke in Quebec.

Armande Saint-Jean: How was it possible for you to escape Rwanda?

Monique Mujawamariya: After the president's plane crashed, I thought to myself, this is the detonator. In March I had felt an oppressive atmosphere. The government soldiers were going out into the street and committing crimes in front of everyone. It boded very ill; we didn't know what exactly, but we felt something coming. I sent my children [a daughter age 20, and two sons, ages 18 and 14] from Kigali [the capital of Rwanda] to the South to visit relatives. [Hutu extremists] were so habitually saying, "We're coming to kill you at such and such an hour," that I thought to myself, I'll do my work as though there's nothing in these threats. If one had listened to them, one would have been changing residences at least four times a day. You were either on the dictator's side, keeping silent about the killings, or else you were against them. But there were human rights violations on both sides, and we were protesting against all of them. Activists felt menaced by both sides.

> It is extremely important that people in the West understand that this is not a fight of Hutus against Tutsis.

On April 7, the day after the crash, the army came to my house to kill me. I had been watching the soldiers all morning, seeing them murder my neighbors one by one. They were killing the women and children inside the houses. All the men were killed in front of my eyes. From the window in my bathroom I followed everything. Then I saw them turn toward my house. I had to hide. I spent a week in the rafters of my house. It was horribly hot. Soldiers camped in my back yard. I told myself that I was going to die of fear.

My servants, whom I considered my friends, stayed with me until the end and helped me escape. On April 12, I finally took advantage of a change of the guard. These soldiers were very, very young. I felt they wouldn't recognize me, they wouldn't know they're supposed to be looking for me. So I asked them to bring me to a hotel in town. They said they would need to go and check with their superior. And then they said his name, and it was the major who'd sworn vengeance on me. I told myself, at least now I know my fate. But the major wasn't around, and the soldiers then asked for money and I agreed to pay them approximately $1,000. It definitely was the most expensive taxi ride of my life! It was arranged that I could take one of the last flights leaving for Brussels. Through the Voice of America, I let my children know that I was safe. But we were separated, without news from each other, for more than three months.

How would you explain the situation in Rwanda?

The people revolted against a well-armed dictatorial regime and they are paying a high price for their attempt to install democracy. The West has a responsibility, because it encouraged the Southern countries to democratize themselves. But during the Cold War, these dictators were overarmed by the West. The dictator's clan knew that, as a result of international pressure and the mobilization of the people, it would have to share power.

> No one spoke to me, not even my mother, because a woman must never leave her husband.

People had massively joined opposition parties; this threw the regime into a fever. So it decided to crush the moderate opposition, to eliminate the intellectuals, to kill everybody who could have laid claim to power.

It is a revolution, within which a genocide has taken place. A genocide is the destruction of human beings for what they are, without any other consideration. In this case, the genocide has been perpetrated by agents of the dictatorial regime against the Tutsi minority. It is extremely important that people in the West understand that this is not a fight of Hutus against Tutsis. It is a fight of a dictator and his militia against the people.

How could human rights activist Agathe Uwilingiyimana [who was killed by Hutu soldiers in April 1994] agree to serve as prime minister in the Habyarimana regime?

In April 1992, opposition parties were so strong that they forced Habyarimana to place key opposition members in high government positions. It was decided that from that point the prime minister would come from the opposition. Two men refused the job because they didn't dare affront Habyarimana. But Agathe felt that it was important to fill the position. She was someone who achieved power without ever thinking about it. She only wanted her country to democratize itself.

Tell us about Rwandan women.

Rwandan women fought for both decolonization and democracy. When men gained the right to vote, women also did. But women are taught to submit to everyone else: their father, their brother, their husband, their mother, everyone. Rwandan women are becoming more mobilized after having been slowed down by traditional culture. Most Rwandans make their living through agricultural work and cooperatives are emerging that are promoting women's economic independence.

I know that you left your husband, who was violent.

It was a slow, painful journey, one that brought me to a crossing in the road. There was a sign there, and on one side was written "Certain Death" and on the other side "Probable Death." Certain death if I stayed with my husband. Probable death if I left, because when I left him I was out of work and I knew that my family would abandon me, which they did for three years. No one spoke to me, not even my mother, because a woman must never leave her husband, even if it means you have to die.

I later found a way to help battered or abandoned women. There are beaten women who stay in their offices; they no longer dare go home or flee to their neighbors, because the neighbors have all started to complain. So what do they do? They pretend to leave for home with the others and come back to sleep underneath their office desk. It's not possible! I swore to myself that I would surely make life better for other women. I invited women to live in my home for three months and helped them find a way to make a living. We had a sort of moral contract whereby each of those women was supposed to do the same for another woman, within a year after leaving my house. And it worked. They did it. So we were creating a substantial network that could bring help to a great number of women.

What does the future hold for Rwanda?

It's unclear whether people will understand that they have all been manipulated. They are victims of a 20-year dictatorship sustained by Western countries. I also reproach our first [postcolonial] politicians, who should have uprooted everything that the Belgians brought with them. I want Rwandans to understand that the Hutu and Tutsi [identity cards] were a colonial method of holding power over us. When the Belgians decided in the 1930s to count Hutus and Tutsis, you know what happened? They could not distinguish one from the other. Outside of the Tutsi royal family there were poor Tutsis; there were also Hutus who were associated with the royal family and therefore more privileged. To be counted as a Tutsi, one had to own five cows. Since the Belgians preferred the Tutsis, everybody wanted to be counted as a Tutsi and many borrowed cows. Only the descendants of the royal family can be sure of their ethnic origin; all the others do not know who their ancestors are. Recent genealogical research has found that many Tutsis have Hutu ancestors and the other way around as well. So these divisions no longer mean anything.

Do you think that the scarcity of resources at the United Nations played a role in the international community's reluctance to intervene in Rwanda?

I think the UN is an outdated institution that has not adapted to the present. It could very well close down and the bureaucrats' pay be used somewhere else. It is amazing that a universal body, created after the world wars, wasn't up to resolving a conflict like this one—in a country as big as a handkerchief. Now that they've gotten themselves into it, it's going to cost them a hundred times more than it would have, if they had permitted the UN force that was already in Kigali to intervene.

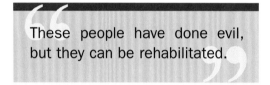

These people have done evil, but they can be rehabilitated.

How can Western countries help now?

Members of the international community are presently concentrating on the task of reconstruction, on the situation of the refugees, on everything that is obvious. They should also pay attention to the fundamental problem— the birth of a just, legal state. If they build only houses, those houses will be destroyed again.

Would you favor a general amnesty?

No, I would identify the sponsors of the genocide and I would throw them in jail for life. But there is a risk of going overboard. I am not in favor of a justice that kills, of capital punishment. There are other punishments that hurt just as much. Death can even be a preferable punishment. The masses of people were carried by the current, people had to obey orders to survive—"Kill him or we kill you." A person becomes an animal. These people have done evil, but they can be rehabilitated.

I would put them to work on public construction sites. They would be given therapy by educators, with supervision by local authorities after their trials. They would be told: rebuild what you have destroyed, although it's impossible to bring the dead back to life. And crime costs a lot. The upkeep of a prisoner, who must be fed, lodged—we don't have the capacity to do it. We're not going to build prisons before building hospitals and schools.

What will happen to the millions of refugees?

They are terribly afraid. But they can be reassured to come back home by an international force that would be well disseminated throughout the country. It must vigorously protect civilians and maintain the peace.

What will the future be for Rwandan women?

Ah, that kills me! When I think of Rwandan women, I see them as the worst victims. When trouble breaks out somewhere, men run away; women look for their children. And in a time of reconstruction, women are disadvantaged because they aren't trained to build roads or houses. The condition of women will deteriorate, even after peace is restored, because they will be left to themselves, with the burden of the elders, the children, even their husband's families to care for. That's how it is. Women need to be priorities for international aid.

Are you planning to go back to Rwanda?

I am going back to set up relief programs and I'll be looking for financing. I'll remain involved in human rights activism, but my main interests now lie in rehabilitation. Even if the fighting stops, there will be two groups of crazy people in Rwanda. One group driven crazy by what they have suffered, and the other group by what they have done and by what they have allowed to happen. I'm working now on the Agathe Uwilingiyimana Foundation, which will provide psychotherapy for young people. Foreign therapists could train teams of Rwandans, for counseling must be done in the native language. Both the killers and the victims must receive therapy close to their communities. But all along the way, we'll be working to bring them together. One day.

Trapped in the Genocide, a Reporter Learns Much About Trust

Lindsey Hilsum

A foreign correspondent on a two-month UN contract was in Kigali, Rwanda's capital city, when the genocide began. She tried to help Rwandans who she knew and worked with, but felt there was little she could do. She continued working as a reporter, trying to convey an understanding of the madness all around her. Finally, she managed to leave the country. It was only later, when she returned to Rwanda, that she learned a shocking truth about the man who guarded her during the time of the killings. Lindsey Hilsum, a freelance journalist, covered Africa for more than a dozen years. She contributes regularly to the *Observer* and BBC4 in Britain.

Evariste was the nightwatchman. He and I were alone in the house in Kigali, the capital of Rwanda, when the killing started. It was on the night of 6 April 1994. A plane carrying the presidents of Rwanda and its neighbouring state Burundi had been shot down, and everybody on board had died. In Kigali, there was confusion. Bands of men armed with machetes, rocks and clubs were roaming the town. Beyond the foliage that enclosed our garden, Kigali shook with rocket-fire and grenade explosions.

I listened to the strokes of Evariste's broom as he swept the terrace at the back of the house. He filled his hours cleaning, making tea and listening to the radio. I was usually on the phone, talking to people elsewhere in Kigali to find out what was going on, and calling London to report.

Every hour or so, I would go out on the terrace, and we would listen to the gunfire and exchange anxious platitudes.

'It's terrible, isn't it?'

'Yes, it's terrible.'

'It sounds as if it's getting worse.'

I tried to open the front gate and look outside. Two soldiers patrolling the dirt road waved their rifles to tell me to get back into the house.

During the day, I was too busy to feel scared. At night, I lay in bed and wondered if I would ever get out of Kigali. Evariste slept outside. Each day started with the crack and sputter of shooting. He showed no fear.

At first—isolated in the house with the taciturn Evariste—I didn't understand that terror lay in the quiet times, when the killers moved undisturbed around the suburbs. . . .

A Job in Rwanda

Why was I there? Because freelance journalism can be an unreliable and therefore varied trade. For the past ten years, I'd worked mainly out of Africa as a reporter. Occasionally, I work for aid agencies in what they call 'emergency countries', where war has brought destitution, hunger and disease. I'd never visited Rwanda. During the 1980s, when I was based in Nairobi, the journalist I met said [Rwanda] was boring—a place where farmers farmed and the government governed. It was the most densely populated country in Africa, more than seven million people trying to live off the land in a country no bigger than Wales. Coffee was its main export. Rwandans were obedient— only the Jehovah's Witnesses refused to perform *umuganda*, the obligatory unpaid communal labour that enabled the government to build a national network of roads, plant forests and construct terraces to contain soil erosion on the hillsides. Aid agencies were well-disposed to Rwanda in those days. President Juvénal Habyarimana's regime was seen as authoritarian, but efficient. Society was so constrained that there was little corruption—if money was provided for clinics, then clinics were built. The Swiss, seeing a society in Africa as disciplined as their own, gave more money to Rwanda than to any other country on the continent.

> "The Rwandans I knew from Unicef . . . were desperate for help."

Last year [1994] I was offered a two-month contract in Rwanda with Unicef, the United Nations Children's Fund. I was to produce a newsletter which was supposed to help the dozens of aid agencies in Rwanda and Burundi work together more effectively, and to help them understand the politics of both countries.

There had, of course, been four years of war. But that had ended in a peace accord, and when I arrived in Kigali in February 1994, two months before the president's plane came down, the country was peaceful except for sporadic grenade attacks and the occasional political assassination. Outside Rwanda, those hardly counted as news. Inside Rwanda, everyone was waiting for something to happen: for political accords to be implemented, for the war to restart, for something to give. . . .

A Close But Distant Relationship Developed

I tried to settle into my rented house. With the foreigner's tact, I had never asked Evariste his *ethnie* [ethnicity] but he was quite tall and slim, with a narrow nose, a typical Tutsi physique, and the owner of the house told me that she believed he was a Tutsi.

Anyway, I scarcely knew him, and his *ethnie* was none of my business. He was simply the nightwatchman. Expatriates and the native rich in Kigali employ watchmen, known as *zammu*, for their houses, as they do all over urban Africa. The wealthy live besieged and guarded by the poor. In Kigali, as crime and shooting increased, the *zammu* learned to open the gate only to whites or to black people who came in cars marked with the symbols of aid agencies. . . .

Evariste and I developed a routine in those few days after the president was killed. I would sleep a few hours at night, after the shooting had died down; at dawn, as the gunfire started up again, I would start work by the telephone. Foreigners were scrambling to leave the country, but I reverted to my role as reporter and stayed.

The killers were murdering people at roadblocks and in their homes. Once a day, Evariste would call a neighbour to try and find out if his wife and two children were still alive.

I thought: their targets are Tutsis. At any moment, they could come for Evariste.

I tried to persuade him to sleep in my absent landlady's bedroom, where I believed he would be safe from the mob, but he refused, saying first that it was not his place to sleep in the bed of *la patronne*, and then that the patrolling soldiers had told all the *zammu* in the neighbourhood to stay outside and keep to their duties, protecting the rich people's houses. The soldiers' authority was greater than mine.

Fragments of news came in by phone for me to piece together and relay to London. A group of men had been to one aid worker's house and demanded that he hand over his Tutsi cook. He refused, but they found the cook and killed him anyway. The prime minister, Agathe Uwilingiyimana, a Hutu, and [a prominent] Tutsi hotel-owner were dead. Ten Belgian UN soldiers had been killed, because Belgium was regarded as pro-RPF [Rwandan Patriotic Front, a Tutsi-led force]; the killers were saying that Belgium was behind the shooting down of the president's plane. The RPF had left their bases in the north and were heading for Kigali.

The Rwandans I knew from Unicef called me from the suburbs. They had abandoned their reserve, the opacity that I'd found so impenetrable in the office, and were desperate for help. One Rwandan colleague, François, was a Hutu, but his son, who was tall like a Tutsi, had lost his ID. 'They said they would kill him, so I gave them the radio, and they spared him. What shall I do when they come again?'

'Give them money bit by bit, don't give them everything at once,' I suggested.

'But there's another problem. They killed my next-door neighbour, Monsieur Albert. They say I was his friend, but it's not true, I didn't really know him. He was Belgian, but I've called the Embassy, and they won't come and get the body. Now the body is beginning to smell.'

'Bury it,' I said. 'It's a health risk.'

'But he's a white man; he should have a proper burial.'

Long after the genocide's end, journalist Lindsey Hilsum learned harsh truths about the night watchman who guarded her in Rwanda. (Gareth Cattermole/Getty Images.)

'It doesn't matter what colour he is; he's dead. Just bury him and say a prayer.'

'But what if the soldiers say I buried him because he was my friend?'

'Tell them you didn't know him, but you had to bury him because of the smell.'

The Situation Was Worsening

François rang back the next day. 'Thank you,' he said. 'I did what you said. You were right. We dug a grave at the front and buried him. Maybe the Belgians will come for him after the war.'

'Maybe they will,' I said, thinking: is this it, is this all I can do? Tell someone to bury a body?

The phone kept ringing. Another colleague, Françoise, rang. She was a classic Tutsi—tall, light-skinned and lithe—one of the women I'd travelled with on the bus to the RPF rally the previous month. Now, she was sobbing hysterically and hiding in a cupboard. Her cousin had been killed on the road outside her house, [and] she knew that her family was next on the list. 'They don't kill you if you give them money and jewellery, but we have given them everything.' She wanted the UN to rescue her, but the UN was evacuating only foreigners.

An RPF contingent had broken out of the old parliament building and had taken on the Presidential Guard; fighting blocked the road to the airport. All the politicians who supported the Arusha Accords were dead or in hiding. A new government had appointed itself.

Soldiers Defeated the Red Cross

I tried to plan how to rescue the people I knew. I was fooling myself—I couldn't do it. Tutsis trying to escape were being pulled from vehicles and slaughtered on the road. I had scarcely any petrol in my car. I didn't know the suburbs where the people lived.

One afternoon, a delegate from the International Red Cross rang. He had seen hundreds, maybe thousands of bodies, evidence of a slaughter far worse than we had imagined. I knew that I had to see for myself if I was to report first hand. The next morning, I drove through the streets, past soldiers swigging beer, and abandoned bodies, to the Red Cross headquarters, and from there, with a medical team, to a Red Cross depot in the suburbs. Two women lay inside, moaning from the pain of bullet wounds. Five bodies lay round the back. Up a hill, two soldiers shifted uneasily outside a house and watched us go in. The bodies of five women lay piled in the flower-bed. Their faces were fixed in terror: flies crawled over the blood of their machete wounds. A woman who had watched from the other side of the valley said that some Tutsis had gathered at the Red Cross depot for safety. In the morning, twenty soldiers had come. Those they did not slaughter on the spot, they marched to the house up the hill and murdered there.

> "The mess spoke of a frenzy of killing, of anger and madness."

In the house, we walked through shards of glass, torn paper, wrecked furniture and broken crockery. The mess spoke of a frenzy of killing, of anger and madness.

We took the wounded to the central hospital. The dying lay two or three to a bed and on the floor, blocking the entrance to the ward. Nurses stepped over them. Blood ran down the steps and along the gutters. Trucks kept arriving, loaded high with more bodies. A woman came into the ward carrying a baby whose leg was partially severed, the tendons and muscles exposed. Relatives patiently told their stories, always the same—Hutu neighbours and soldiers had thrown grenades in their house because they were Tutsis.

That night, after we left, the soldiers went into the wards and finished off most of the patients.

Leaving Rwanda

I went back to the house. Evariste was still there. The next morning, after a sleepless night, I went into the living-room, sat down and started to cry.

Evariste sat silently opposite me. Eventually, he said, in French, 'Why are you crying, Madame?'

'Because I'm scared,' I replied. He waited.

'Don't be scared,' he said, at last.

I told him I would have to leave; I couldn't stay much longer in the house because the telephone would soon be cut off and, without the telephone, I couldn't work. I needed to go to the hotel where other journalists were. But I didn't want to abandon him. To Evariste, the answer was simple.

> 'You are a European; you should be with other Europeans.'

'You are a European; you should be with other Europeans,' he said.

The UN security officer, a flamboyant French former policeman known by his radio call-sign, 'Moustache,' was driving around town with a single armed guard rescuing foreigners. When he asked his headquarters in New York if he could help Rwandan UN staff, he was told no. He had no support from the UN troops because they had retreated to barracks. Two months earlier, when all UN staff had been asked to mark their house on a map in case of emergency, I had decided not to bother. In case of emergency, I might want to stay. Now I rang Moustache.

'At last you ring me!' he said. 'Tell me where you are and I am coming for you.'

He took me to a house where, as Evariste had predicted, I found other Europeans. Other journalists began to arrive, and I moved into a hotel. After a few more days, I left Kigali for Nairobi, and then Nairobi for Burundi, where I would go to the border to meet the first refugees heading south, away from the charnel house Rwanda had become. . . .

A Shocking Conclusion

The last time I went to Kigali, I looked for people who had known Evariste. By the time [Oxfam staffer] Esther Mujawayo took me to meet a driver who had news of him, I had guessed what the news would be. The driver told me he had crossed a roadblock near the house where I had stayed about a week after the killing started and had seen Evariste on one of the barricades.

'What was he doing?' I asked.

'He was carrying a gun.'

'Could he have been forced to do it?'

'They only gave guns to certain people, those they trusted. He was with them—he was one of them. We know that.'

The driver, who was a Tutsi, faced death as he approached the roadblock. He pretended that he was employed by the Belgian Red Cross. 'Evariste didn't look at me, and I didn't look at him. I pretended not to know him, but I saw him.'

I wondered whether Evariste had waited until I left before beginning his work, or whether he had already started, those nights when he refused to sleep inside the house. I wondered what deals he had done with the soldiers outside. What had he been thinking, why did he do it, what did it mean to him? Had he been a member of the *interahamwe* [Hutu paramilitary] before, or did it start then? Was he forced or did he believe in what he was doing? I wondered at how I could not have known, at my foolishness, at my painful ignorance, at my inability to understand or just to see. The days we had spent together in the house in Kigali had been the most terrifying of my life. I had been through all that with Evariste, yet I had known nothing of him, nor his people, nor where he came from, nor how he felt and thought.

A Rwandan Woman Endures Years as a Refugee

Marie Béatrice Umutesi

Marie Béatrice Umutesi fled Rwanda with her family when the killing began. In this selection, she describes life in one of the better refugee camps in Zaire, not far from the Rwanda border. She describes the lack of food and difficult conditions in the camp. Violence—whether motivated by vengeance, suspicion, or money—was a common occurrence. Umutesi was born in Rwanda in 1959. A sociologist, she worked in rural development in Rwanda and then, after the genocide, in Cameroon.

Once every two weeks we received enough corn, either as grain or flour, as well as beans or lentils, salt, and oil to survive for a week at most.

SOURCE. Marie Béatrice Umutesi, *Surviving the Slaughter: The Ordeal of a Rwandan Refugee in Zaire*. Madison, WI: University of Wisconsin Press, 2000. Translation copyright © 2000 by The Board of Regents of the University of Wisconsin System. Reproduced by permission.

Malnutrition was rampant among children under five and among pregnant and nursing mothers, particularly those who lived alone and did not have the opportunity to hire themselves out to the locals. Among the many children with bloated stomachs, huge heads, and frail limbs whom I met every day at the nutrition center at INERA [a refugee camp in Zaire], I remember Muhawe, my little four-year-old neighbor. His mother had died on the way to Zaire while giving birth to his little sister. The baby had only survived her mother by a few days, and Muhawe now lived with his widowed grandmother. When Muhawe left Rwanda, he was a chubby three-year-old. Bad food and dysentery had made him into a little old man whose huge head was all you noticed. He was too weak to get up and walk even a few steps and just sat in front of his grandmother's *blindé* [shelter]. To go back inside, he crawled on his hands and knees like a baby. His grandmother brought him regularly to the nutritional center, but the diet he was given didn't have much of an effect. He either vomited it all up or else refused to swallow. When I arrived in the neighborhood, Muhawe had reached an advanced state of malnutrition. To save him, we had to find meals with meat, the only thing he still was willing to swallow and that didn't cause him to vomit. Unfortunately, the nutrition center didn't give him any, and the grandmother was too poor to buy any, even once a week. I therefore began to feed this little boy myself and prepared meals with vegetables and potatoes and made him eat them first before getting a piece of meat, in spite of his tears and nausea. The first days were the most difficult, but later he ate everything I gave him without my having to force him.

I was happy to see him get stronger and be able to cross the distance between his grandmother's *blindé*

> One day when I was on the verge of cracking, I took a pen and began to write down everything that was in my heart.

and mine alone, but rebellion gnawed at me. What had Muhawe and the thousands or other Rwandan children who were dying in the camps done? Was Muhawe guilty of genocide to deserve this fate? Why was he condemned to die? One day when I was on the verge of cracking, I took a pen and began to write down everything that was in my heart. I described the suffering of Muhawe and the other children, who, like him, were starving and whose graves lined the long road into exile. I described the tragedy of the old women who lived alone in plastic *blindés* riddled with holes, and the suffering of the street children of Bukavu who lived by begging. I imagined the horror experienced by the young RPF [Rwandan Patriotic Front, a Tutsi-led force] soldier who, back from the war, found that the militias had exterminated his entire family. I spoke of the murder of my cousin Laurent and my mother's friend Nyirarukwavu. I made a habit of writing so that people could know and break their silence, but also to stop my own pain. I often wept while I wrote, but when I had finished I felt comforted.

Survival Was Cruel

To deal with the lack of food aid, many of my neighbors went to work for the locals. In return they received cassava, bananas, and a little money. For a day's work they earned on average the equivalent of twenty-five cents in American money. I happened to run into old school friends who had to work for a couple of beer bananas to provide some variety in their families' diet. Women, who in Rwanda had been civil servants or had worked in the private sector and who had left beautiful houses and cars in Kigali [the capital of Rwanda], allowed themselves to be insulted by potential employers because the survival of their families was at

> The number of women raped while gathering firewood in the plantations of Zaire is incalculable.

stake. Some locals took advantage of the abundance of female workers to force the women to sleep with them prior to hiring them. Some, particularly those who had sole responsibility for their families, accepted this and a few months later found themselves pregnant, with no possibility of terminating these undesired pregnancies. In addition to working for the locals, women planted kitchen gardens in the spaces between the *blindés*. The sight of this greenery brightened up the misery. Other economic activities such as small businesses, production of banana beer and corn fritters, basketwork and carpentry took place in the camps. Those with a little money even opened small restaurants, boutiques, butcher shops, cafes, sewing ateliers, hair dressing salons, and so forth.

The provisions of heating wood from the humanitarian organizations were also insufficient, and a week's ration lasted at most three or four days. As a result, the refugees went to the Zairian eucalyptus plantations to make up this deficit, which contributed to tensions among the two communities. Men risked being beaten to death if they were caught, but women were in greater danger. They ran more slowly than the men and weren't strong enough to defend themselves when they were caught. The number of women raped while gathering firewood in the plantations of Zaire is incalculable.

Violence Was Part of Everyday Life

In addition to the practical problems, we were confronted with constant threats to our safety. The great majority of Hutu of all classes had left Rwanda when the rebels took power. This meant that in the camps bandits, ministers, bankers, assassins, businessmen, simple peasants, and soldiers lived side by side, and victims lived with those who had persecuted them in times past. I often met Braddock, the young soldier who, at Kigali, had forced us to bring him tea every morning at the roadblock. He had become a refugee in rags, like so many others. Without a gun to make himself important, he had returned to being the young delinquent he had been before the war, no longer the feared killer who had made us tremble. One day he begged money for food from me. Even unarmed he was a potential danger and his presence in the area didn't make me feel secure. I knew what he was capable of doing for a little money.

The presence of weapons was another factor in this insecurity. The disarmament had worked well enough, but not every little street had been searched. There were people with weapons and grenades everywhere. The situation was most dangerous in the camps of Panzi and Bulonge, where there was a large concentration of soldiers. Grenades exploded there every night and in the morning you mourned the dead, victims of jealousy or account settling. In other places this happened too, but less regularly. My uncle barely escaped death at Panzi. A grenade had been tossed into his *blindé*. His wife escaped unharmed, but his arm was mangled. At any rate, with the continuing impoverishment of the refugees, those who had weapons began to sell them to the Zairian military and the Burundian rebels. These sales, dictated by the need to survive, solved the problem of weapons. The last year there were almost no deaths caused by firearms or grenades.

> After a few hours the shooting stopped, but we had lost interest in our meeting.

Repeated attacks by soldiers from the RPF were an additional cause of uncertainty and created a state of generalized psychosis. The camp at Birava, located on the shores of Lake Kivu, across from Rwanda, was attacked at the beginning of 1995 by a commando group made up of about one hundred Rwandan soldiers supported by mortars located on a small Zairian island in Lake Kivu. More than sixty people were killed with grenades, mortars, and knives and more than a hundred others were wounded. Following this attack the camp at Birava was deserted. The camp at Panzi was also the target of regular attacks from Rwanda. Twice, when shooting broke out, I was at Panzi. The first time, I was presiding over a meeting of women delegates from the camps in South Kivu, making preparations for International Women's Day on March 8, 1995. At first we attempted to keep calm and I continued to moderate the debates as if nothing [was] happening. Then someone called out that it would be better to take shelter and we rushed to the hall, since the meeting room had large bay windows. Bullets whistled above us. After a few hours the shooting stopped, but we had lost interest in our meeting. After this experience, I didn't want to take the risk of going to Panzi again. Nevertheless, a year later, pressured by the women's organization there, I had to return. What a mistake! Around three o'clock, I began to hear the sound of machine gun fire. As we were close to a Zairian police station, I thought the noise came from there and wasn't worried. Another woman commented that the "Rwandan music" was starting but she didn't seem to attach too much importance to it either. In the marketplace it was business as usual. A few minutes later, however, the shooting became louder. The market emptied in no time. The *blindés* emptied too. Everyone ran to the ground floors of buildings or to houses with concrete roofs. Around five o'clock the gunfire stopped and I was able to go home. Every attack on a camp by the RPF was followed by a period of generalized fear, even in the camps that had not been targets.

Killings Motivated by Vengeance, Fear, and Money

Suspicion and fear themselves created insecurity. When an unknown person entered a camp, he was in danger of being lynched. Often it was enough for someone to simply shout that someone was RPF for him to be killed. Even the employees of the humanitarian NGOs [nongovernmental organizations] were threatened. Camps like Kashusha, where there was a large concentration of bandits from Kigali, were among the most dangerous. A friend of mine and her sister were very nearly lynched when they returned from visiting me. They left at about six o'clock, and when they got to the Bukavu-Goma road, which separated INERA from Kashusha, two strangers began to follow them, and they began to run. At the taxi stand they slowed down. The two crooks started to yell, "Catch the rebels" and pointed at them. They found themselves surrounded by menacing onlookers. The robbers took advantage of the situation to steal their watches and glasses. A passerby who recognized them saved them from being lynched. If you wanted to appropriate someone else's possessions, you only had to accuse them of being RPF. By this simple word you could activate a blind killing machine, guided only by fear, resentment, and vengeance, though as time passed these feelings diminished.

At INERA, I was considered to be "pro-RPF" because, among other things, I looked like a Tutsi and had a Tutsi name, and I preferred the company of the old women in my neighborhood to that of the directors of the camp. They also held it against me that I organized meetings in my *blindé* without permission. INERA was organized by Father Carlos of Caritas-Spain, who ran the camp with a firm hand, and lynching, possible at Kashusha, was impossible at INERA. Nevertheless I was afraid, particularly when people came by my *blindé* asking if this [was] the place where the RPF woman lived. It was so easy to place a grenade in a *blindé*. All you needed to do was cut the sheeting near the bed with a razor and put the grenade next to the sleeper, and it was all over. Some days I had trouble sleeping. I wouldn't have been the first woman to be killed by a grenade. About five hundred meters from me, a grenade had killed a young woman and a little girl, and a visiting priest had lost an arm. The assassins were never found. Another family that had escaped death lived in the "prefects" neighborhood. Around two in the morning the woman heard a noise, and she awakened her husband. They got up to see if someone had entered the sheeting to steal. They lit a light and saw that the sheeting had been cut in several places, but everything seemed to be in order. The neighbors, who had heard them speaking, came over to hear the news. The woman got up with her baby in her arms, but as it was cold outside she went back inside to get a cover from the bed to wrap around the baby. It was dark in the *blindé*. While groping around for the cover, she felt something round and cold. She called her husband to bring a flashlight. They discovered a grenade with the pin half out. If it had fallen on the floor it would have exploded.

The deterioration of conditions in the camps brought with it another type of criminality. Killings, for vengeance or out of fear, began to give way to killings committed for the purpose of robbery. A priest who was visiting his parents was killed in Kashusha camp and robbed of two thousand American dollars. While walking around the camp one evening, to see for himself what the reality of life there was, he was approached by a well-known bandit, Pariti, and his gang. The next morning they found his body in the camp cemetery. In Mudaka camp a young man tried to strangle his friend with a rope for a hundred American dollars. Neighbors who heard him yelling intervened and saved him. Security was precarious, and the numbers of rapes, killings, and robberies stayed relatively high despite the introduction of new efforts to maintain order.

Rwandan Children Tell How They Escaped

Julienne Kampogo, Delphine Uwituze, and Augustin Nshimiyimana

About a decade after the genocide, three young Rwandans from different families explained what happened to them. While many of their relatives died, each survived through combinations of cunning, chance, daring, the help of others, and their faith. Afterward, largely alone and deeply affected by the massacres, each has tried to come to terms with a new reality. These selections were taken from *Stars of Rwanda: Children Write and Draw about Their Experiences During the Genocide of 1994*. The editor of that book, Wiljo Woodi Oosterom, is the founder of Silent Work, a self-help aid agency she operates in Africa and the Netherlands.

SOURCE. Julienne Kampogo, Delphine Uwituze, Augustin Nshimiyimana, *Stars of Rwanda: Children Write and Draw about Their Experiences During the Genocide of 1994*. Amsterdam: Silent Work Foundation, 2004. Copyright © 2004 Silent Work Foundation. Reproduced by permission.

The Experience of Julienne Kampogo

My name is Julienne Kampogo. I am a survivor of the 1994 Rwandan genocide. My father, mother, brothers and sisters were killed. Witnessing the genocide gave me an extraordinary strength that enabled me to help people regardless of their ethnic background. As a Christian I was pushed to act accordingly and my faith in God helped me to go on until the end. . . .

I was born in an extended family of about one thousand people, but only a handful of them have survived. The morning of the 4th of April 1994 my parents and I said goodbye to each other without knowing that it was our last time to meet.

> I made a decision to sacrifice myself for those who were to be massacred.

7th April 1994 was the memorable date on which the evil befell our country and people died en masse. In a period of three months, over one million innocent people lost their lives. Most of those killed were from my ethnic group (Tutsi) but there were also moderate Hutus who were not in favour of the genocide plan. Killers used various forms of torture in such a way that it was a blessing to be shot by a gunman, but you had to pay a large amount of money! Even those who were proponents of human rights protection perished in this hell.

On the very date when our neighbours were killed, we were prepared to be executed like them. One of us (we were together in a hiding place) who was not targeted to be killed as we were, left us and we hoped he would come back to protect us. There were seven of us and two were not "destined to be killed," but the remaining five were hunted down to be exterminated. I made a decision to sacrifice myself for those who were to be massacred.

We were betrayed on 12th April 1994, though the killers already knew that we were in the house. They decided to come to kill us. Two militia men came over and ordered us to go outside to be shot. Fortunately I knew one of the two, and I asked him how much I could give them in exchange for our lives and they accepted the 50,000 Frs (it was all we had). He became a bit "compassionate" and asked me if it was the only money I had and when I nodded my head saving yes, he gave me back 5,000 Frs.

> We put ourselves in God's hands with prayers which He answered!

Our stomachs were empty and I had to do something for the others. I took them to a room and closed it; it was only open when I went there to feed them or during the time of prayer. We used to pray three times a day. We fasted on Tuesdays and Fridays. With the 5,000 Frs left by the militia, I bought maize flour. I had to climb a wall of a neighbouring house using a chair and a drain-pipe as a ladder to get some vegetables in the neighbour's garden. I had to work fast because the area was guarded by fierce dogs which ate dead human bodies.

Our persecution took long and the soldiers came back to ask me if I knew the five young men really well. I told them that they were innocent; if I hadn't said this, it would have been a death sentence for me and them. Thank God our lives were spared.

The war to stop the genocide continued and bullets from both sides (RPF, the Rwandese Patriotic Front soldiers and Rwandan forces of the time) reached our hiding place. By God's grace, no one was injured at the time. We put ourselves in God's hands with prayers which He answered! When we opened the Bible, our eyes saw from time to time the comforting verses such as Psalms 90/91. It felt like an endless war, though it probaby lasted a short time in terms of months.

After a long time, the other person who left us without protection came back in our hiding place. He asked me to flee with him on condition that I leave behind those people under my protection. I refused that offer.

Two soldiers came and told me it was better to leave. I could not give in and leave my protégés.

I opened my Bible and came across a verse saying that, "Whoever abides on his life will lose it and whoever loses his life for others will get it." From that moment, it was impossible for me to leave behind those poor young men. I was the only one who could go out to fetch food.

> At 9.00 A.M. the militia came to execute us.

God's providence sent us a car which took us to St. Paul's centre (a Catholic Church conference centre). That was our only hope for survival. When we reached the place, I asked those youths to continue hiding themselves; the killers had sworn to kill us after they had killed all the others. There in St. Paul we happened to meet other people with whom we shared the same fate. Many have died, others were casualties. My life of self-giving continued even there. There was no medical assistance; I was using water to clean the terrible wounds of the girls and women while one of my protégés was doing the same for the men.

We did not know that God was planning our rescue. The RPF army struggled to keep us out of the bands of the killers. At the same time the militia multiplied their assaults to kill us before the RPF came for our liberation. The liberating army reached us around 3.00 A.M. They told us that they had found a safe place for us at some distance from the battlefield. Many people followed them. Due to the fact that I was looking after those causalities, I could not go away leaving them behind helpless.

At 9.00 A.M. the militia came to execute us; we went to a hiding place where we could take the wounded people, both Hutus and Tutsis, and I asked them not to consider their differences because they were all victims of the war. I rather begged them to pray hard. At 4.00 P.M. local time, a good-hearted police officer helped us to take refuge in another place called St. Michel (the Kigali Archdiocese Cathedral parish). There were various people: religious nuns, brothers, priests and lay people. That night we slept on the bare cement, all alike.

Early in the morning, without worrying about the noise of bullets, a benevolent priest went to look for mattresses while others volunteered to find food for the whole community. Throughout the night we carried on our unceasing prayers, including the Eucharistic celebration also done in silence.

At about 3.00 A.M. on the 4th [of] July 1994, the RPF soldiers came for our final liberation. They stood near us and said to us: "Peace be with you." Thank God we were free from death! . . .

The Experience of Delphine Uwituze

In our family, before the war, we were with five children. I was the second born. As a young child, I saw my elder sisters and the children of our neighbours go to school and I wanted to follow them. I was sad because that was not possible. My parents consoled me by telling me that I would go when the time came. When the right time came, I was brought to a nursery school. When the first school year was ended, instead of being promoted to the following class in the nursery school, I was taken directly to the primary school. I tried to cope with the situation despite the fact that I was still very young then, but because of high marks and my rank (average 98% being the first in my class), I was promoted to the second class of primary school. I was always the first of my class.

Before the war, we were neither poor nor rich. My father was working in a sub-Prefecture and my mother was a member of parliament from 1988 until 1992. Our parents cherished us very much and often brought

> My daddy was taken to a place called Golgatha, where they stripped him of his nice clothes, which they put on, and killed him on the spot.

us nice gifts such as clothes, shoes, bread, biscuits, chocolates, fritters, cakes, sweets and so on. When my mother came back from Europe she brought us precious gifts.

During the war, the situation became very bad; our mother was hated because she was no longer a member of parliament. She had been fired under the pretext that her mandate was over while she had done nothing palpable and beneficial for them.

In 1993 a young man was living with our family for whom my father was godfather. One year later, the genocide started. During the night we heard people beating on the iron sheets of the roof of our neighbour's house. My daddy, my mummy and the other boy went out to check what was going on, [and] they found two fierce men who were living in our neighbourhood. "What is happening?" my mother asked. "Don't you know what is going on either? If you are not careful, we can chop your head off," they answered. We could hear the cries of people running for shelter all night long.

The following morning, our mum clothed us with as many garments as possible and she took our provision of tea in a thermos, some bread in a blue carrier bag and she took us to her friends up country. Our mother left us there and went back home, where our daddy, his godson and two houseworkers were. Then, there appeared two strange men dressed in shabby clothes and armed with machetes and swords, [and] they had an order to take my father with them. After they took him, they came back and told the young man to go with them so that they could show him where his godfather was. My daddy was taken to a place called Golgotha, where they stripped him of his nice clothes, which they put on, and killed him on the spot.

Together with some other people, my mummy had hidden somewhere in the bush. Somebody found out where they were hidden; it was not far from his house. When the secret of the hiding place was discovered they

Children Show Positive Attitudes

Twelve years after the genocide, 72 percent of Rwandan children said they were happy. Of the 72 percent, about half were happy "most of the time" and the other half "sometimes."

These were among the findings in a 2006 report by UNICEF and the African Child Policy Forum, which surveyed 514 Rwandans age nine to seventeen.

Half of the children said people sometimes scream at each other in their homes, and a quarter said there were, rarely or occasionally, beatings at home.

But 94 percent were "optimistic that they will have a better life than their parents are currently leading," the report said.

made a plan to kill them and to burn all my mother's belongings. One man from the group of killers dressed in banana leaves camouflage knew my mother and advised her to flee from that place because another more dangerous group from Kibungo would soon come with handgrenades and heavy guns.

Our mother came to take us, we collected a few things and went to seek refuge. When we reached a certain place, we saw many people who looked like wild beasts. One of them entered and asked my mum: "Come with me to explain what you have done." That man was carrying [a] lot of bottles; my mother explained that they were not really bottles but grenades.

Suddenly, those who were in the same hiding place with mummy left and ran away. The killers pursued them. That was our chance to flee, this time we all went in different directions.

When the war was over and the RPF soldiers came, we could go back to our home. We found the house destroyed. Its windows, doors and ceiling board all broken. The house was empty because everything had been looted except two metallic doors of the living room that were too heavy; that's why they were spared.

We stayed at home for a couple of days, but I went to live at my aunt's place to go to my class in our school. When I reached primary six I maintained my rank of being the first of our class; I had subsequently 91% at the end of the first term, 93% in the second term and during the third term I fell sick, but I still did my exam being sick but they gave me an opportunity to succeed, this time with 69% average.

> Our life is miserable: We are unable to go to school, there's no medical treatment.

I was sent for further studies to Butare. In my new school, I made an effort to study hard. After the second term I got 86% although I was sick, still being the second of the class. In short I am struggling to be the first if God wishes.

My wish after my secondary school education is to go to University abroad. I want to become a researcher. . . .

The Experience of Augustin Nshimiyimana

I went to primary school at Mulinga from 1986 until 1990. I attended a vocational training centre (technical school), which I was not able to finish after I studied there for two years. Because of my parents' poverty and lack of schooling, I stayed in the village with my four brothers and sisters, helping them to cultivate our almost barren fields. I lived this kind of life until 1994, when the genocide started.

The genocide war in Rwanda started in April 1994 and lasted until 20th July 1994. I was with two of my siblings; we missed our parents who had fled with the other two children, but we found them later.

We went to a shelter at the Busoro river where we spent a whole week. When we went to fetch water and came back, we met people who had fled with our parents, leaving us behind, because of the battle that took place there.

Even now I have no idea of their whereabouts, whether they are dead or alive is still a question without an answer for me.

Now, I am still living with two brothers who survived the genocide together with me, the eldest. Our life is miserable: We are unable to go to school, there's no medical treatment. We are living in a rented room for which we have to pay 5,000 Frw per month. I am doing some petty business with the 50,000 Frw as my capital and we have to pay 10,000 Frw rent. My two brothers depend on me for everything.

When I analyse the situation, I find that I try to solve problems beyond my reach. I didn't get help from anybody; I sweated blood and tears to get that small capital.

Since 1995, I was working as a houseboy and discovered that my young brothers weren't any help to the point that they were almost turning into street boys because they had no one to look after them. I decided to quit my job and dedicate my life to my brothers. First, I carried a box in which I put some things to sell on the street. It was quite risky for me because those who are in charge of security from time to time took those things away from me because it is illegal. That is why I found that it was better to hire a permanent place for that business.

If I could find a benefactor who can support me, I can increase my capital and earn more money for a house, enough food, and the children can go to school. In so doing, I can continue the obligation of my parental care for my brothers.

CHRONOLOGY

1300s	Tutsis enter the territory of what is now Rwanda where Twas and Hutus already reside.
1600s–1800s	Tutsi kings consolidate power.
1890	Germany makes Rwanda part of German East Africa.
1916	During World War I, Belgian troops take over Rwanda and retain control after Germany loses the war.
1921	Rwanda and neighboring Burundi become Belgian colonies, with power delegated to a Tutsi king in each, although Tutsis make up only about 15 percent of the population. Almost all the rest are Hutus.
1926–1931	Belgium begins issuing identity cards that differentiate Tutsis and Hutus. The card policy continues into 1994.
1946	After the end of World War II and the formation of the United Nations, Rwanda becomes a UN trust territory administered by Belgium.
1959	The last Tutsi king dies under suspicious circumstances. Hutus rebel against Belgian and Tutsi control. More than 100,000 Tutsis flee to Burundi and other countries.
1962	Belgium withdraws and Rwanda and Burundi become independent countries. The first president of Rwanda is a Hutu, Grégoire Kayibanda. Violence forces more Tutsis to flee Rwanda, but they remain in power in Burundi.

1963–1967	Tutsis launch attacks into Rwanda from Burundi; Hutus kill thousands.
1973	In a military coup, a Hutu officer, Juvénal Habyarimana, replaces Kayibanda as president. Subsequently, under his one-party government, Tutsis are excluded from most government and military jobs.
1990	Armed men from a Tutsi-run organization, the Rwandan Patriotic Front (RPF), invade Rwanda from Uganda. The Rwandan army begins training and equipping Hutu civilian militias. Fighting continues for several years, despite a 1991 cease-fire agreement.
1993	With French encouragement, President Habyarimana and the RPF sign a peace agreement (the Arusha accords) calling for a coalition Hutu-RPF government. About 2,500 UN troops arrive in the capital, Kigali, to help with the accords, but by the following April all but 300 are withdrawn. Tensions rise.
April 6, 1994	Habyarimana, president since 1973, and the president of Burundi, Cyprien Ntaryamira, are killed when Habyarimana's plane is shot down near the Kigali airport. The party responsible for attacking the plane is never determined, but anti-accord extremists are believed to be involved. That night, the genocide starts.
April 7, 1994	Rwandan troops and civilian militias begin killing Tutsis and moderate Hutus, including Prime Minister Agathe Uwilingiyimana. The RPF launches a counter-attack.
April–August 1994	Hundreds of thousands of people, primarily Tutsis but also many moderate Hutus, are slaughtered. More than a million other Rwandans—Hutus and Tutsis—flee to neighboring countries. Tens of thousands of refugees

die of cholera, and many others are killed by ethnic conflict in refugee camps in 1994 and over the next two years.

May 17, 1994	As the genocide continues, the UN decides to send 6,800 troops and policemen to Rwanda to defend civilians, but deployment is delayed because of arguments over who will pay the cost.
July 4, 1994	The RPF captures Kigali and the Hutu government flees. The Hutu extremists succeed with the genocide, but then lose control of the country. Subsequently, Tutsi forces pursue and kill Hutu refugees.
November 8, 1994	With the agreement of the new Rwandan government, the UN Security Council establishes a tribunal to prosecute those involved in the genocide.
December 1995	The UN genocide tribunal announces its first indictments, against eight suspects. Trials begin a year later.
November 1996	As a mass return of refugees begins, the Rwandan government orders a moratorium on arrests of suspected genocide perpetrators.
2000	The Rwandan parliament ratifies Paul Kagame, an RPF leader, as president.
2001–2002	With the country's judiciary decimated, the government commissions tribal courts, known as *gacacas*, to involve citizens in trials of genocide suspects.
2003	The first national election since the genocide confirms Kagame as president.

FOR FURTHER READING

Books

Howard Adelman and Astri Suhrke, eds., *The Path of a Genocide: The Rwanda Crisis from Uganda to Zaire*. New Brunswick, NJ: Transaction Publishers, 1999.

Michael Barnett, *Eyewitness to Genocide: The United Nations and Rwanda*. Ithaca, NY: Cornell University Press, 2002.

Roméo Dallaire, *Shake Hands with the Devil: The Failure of Humanity in Rwanda*. Toronto: Random House Canada, 2003.

Alison Des Forges, *Leave None to Tell the Story: Genocide in Rwanda*. New York: Human Rights Watch, 1999.

Alain Destexhe, *Rwanda and Genocide in the Twentieth Century*, translated by Alison Marschner. New York University Press, 1995.

Philip Gourevitch, *We Wish to Inform You That Tomorrow We Will Be Killed with Our Families*. New York: Farrar, Straus and Giroux, 2005.

Jean Hatzfeld, *The Antelope's Strategy: Living in Rwanda After the Genocide*. Translated by Linda Coverdale. New York: Farrar, Straus and Giroux, 2007.

Jean Hatzfeld, *Machete Season: The Killers in Rwanda Speak*. Translated by Linda Coverdale. New York: Farrar, Straus and Giroux, 2005.

Alan J. Kuperman, *The Limits of Humanitarian Intervention: Genocide in Rwanda*. Washington, DC: Brookings Institution Press, 2001.

Ian Linden, *Church and Revolution in Rwanda*. Manchester, U.K.: Manchester University Press, 1977.

Mahmood Mamdani, *When Victims Become Killers: Colonialism, Nativism, and the Genocide in Rwanda*. Princeton, NJ: Princeton University Press, 2002.

Linda Melvern, *A People Betrayed: The Role of the West in Rwanda's Genocide*. London: Zed Press, 2000.

Rakiya Omaar and Alex de Waal, *Rwanda: Death, Despair and Defiance*, 2nd ed. London: African Rights, 1995.

Samantha Power, *A Problem from Hell: America and the Age of Genocide*. New York: Basic Books, 2002.

Gerard Prunier, *The Rwanda Crisis: History of a Genocide*. New York: Columbia University Press, 1995.

Andre Sibomana, *Hope for Rwanda*. Sterling, VA: Pluto Press, 1999.

Periodicals

Arthur Asiimwe, "Rwanda Accuses France Directly over 1994 Genocide," *Reuters*, August 5, 2008.

Bill Clinton, "U.S. Assistance to Rwandan Refugees," *U.S. Department of State Dispatch*, vol. 5, issue 32, August 8, 1994.

Economist, "Genocide in Rwanda," vol. 331, no. 7864, May 21, 1994.

Kevin Fedarko, "Rwanda: The Swagger of Defeat," *Time*, August 15, 1994.

P. Geltman and E. Stover, "Genocide and the Plight of Children in Rwanda," *Journal of the American Medical Association*, vol. 227, 1997.

Richard Grenier, "Western Ideals Aren't Found in Killing Field," *Insight on the News*, vol. 10, no. 21, May 23, 1994.

Helen Hintjens, "Intimate Enemy: Images and Voices of the Rwanda Genocide," *Ethnic and Racial Studies*, vol. 30, no. 4, July 2007.

Douglas Jehl, "U.S. Policy: A Mistake; Tragedy in Rwanda Seen as Preventable," *New York Times*, July 23, 1994.

Jean Baptiste Kayigamba, "Rwandans Not About to Forget Clinton's Words," *Inter Press Service*, March 26, 1998.

Sam Kiley, "The Horrific Scars of Rwanda's Civil War," *U.S. News & World Report*, vol. 117, no. 1, July 4, 1994.

Mahmood Mandami, "Footsteps of Hutu-Tutsi Killings," *New Vision*, September 4, 1995.

James Martin, "Media Camouflage," *America*, vol. 171, issue 5, August 27, 1994.

Marguerite Michaels, "Sorry, Wrong Country," *Time*, vol. 143, no. 23, June 6, 1994.

Catharine Newbury, "Background to Genocide in Rwanda," *Issue*, vol. 23, no. 2, 1995.

New York Times, "Horror in Rwanda, Shame in the UN," May 3, 1994.

Thomas J. O'Hara, "Rwandan Bishops Faltered in Face of Crisis; Hierarchical Church Seen Too Close to Regime," *National Catholic Reporter*, vol. 31, no. 42, September 29, 1995.

Elizabeth Levy Patrick, "The Media and the Rwanda Genocide," *African Study Review*, vol. 52, no. 1, April 2009.

Eric Ransdell, "The Wounds of War," *U.S. News & World Report*, vol. 117, no. 21, November 28, 1994.

David Rieff, "An Age of Genocide," *New Republic*, vol. 214, no. 5, January 29, 1996.

D.N. Smith, "The Genesis of Genocide in Rwanda," *Humanity and Society*, vol. 19, no. 4, 1995.

Frank Smith, "Cashing in on Rwanda's Genocide," *New Statesman and Society*, vol. 7, no. 313, July 29, 1994.

Alan Thompson, "On Trial for Rwanda's Genocide," *World Press Review*, vol. 45, no. 5, May 1998.

INDEX

V